INNOVATION

This book is dedicated to Alvin P. Lehnerd.

Innovation:
The Workbook

Marc H. Meyer & Frederick G. Crane

The Institute for Enterprise Growth
Boston, Massachusetts

For information:
info@instituteforenterprisegrowth.com

Book Title: Innovation: The Workbook
Printed in the United States of America
Library of Congress Cataloging-in-Publication Data
Innovation: The Workbook/ Marc H. Meyer, Frederick G. Crane.
ISBN 978-1-329-74910-8 (pbk. : acid-free paper)
1. Entrepreneurship. 2. Innovation. 3. Business planning.
4. Business models. 5. Venture finance.

CONTENTS

ACKNOWLEDGEMENTS

We have crafted the methods in Innovation: The Workbook from our own direct experience in startups and in larger corporations creating new products, systems, and services. We like to think of these as next generation solutions because in all these cases, we have focused on applications for new users or new uses with different types of technology. This has not only led to new product or service designs, but often, enhanced business models to propel the innovations forward into the marketplace.

These methods are derived from lots of experience and what some might consider decades of hard work. But in fact, that work has often not really felt like work at all. If you too get hooked on innovation, you will feel the same way.

The challenge in writing this book has been to make innovation more systematic – to not rely just on a random "Aha!" but rather, to follow a set of systematic methods which over time, produce a stream of insights and new designs, e.g. a bunch of Aha's. That is what we have tried to do here – to offer you a simple yet robust set of methods that get the job done so that anyone, young or old, new to the game or highly experienced, can innovate with and on behalf of customers.

Our heartfelt thanks go to Arjan Friedericks, a visiting scholar to Northeastern from the Netherlands, who proofed and tested every chapter with his students. And just as important to this effort was Kaylan Tran, our graphic designer. We are also grateful to Johnny Fayad and Ali Kothari, co-founders of New Ground Foods, and Abby Titcomb, founder of Knightly – student entrepreneurs whose ventures are examples in the book. And we extend our gratitude to the entire Northeastern IDEA team who have applied and improved these methods to hundreds of new companies over the past five years.

This book is dedicated to Al Lehnerd, a legend in industry for his unconventional thinking, humor, and numerous product and business innovations. Most consider Al the father of product platforming — a topic you will be learning in this book. We continue to learn from him. And Al's teaching is the type that goes beyond the artifact of a new product or system and into the deeper meaning of teamwork, continuous learning, and having the courage to simply do the right thing even when it is not easy or popular to do so.

Be a pioneer. Be bold, be different, but at the same time, be practical in your thinking. As George Patton, the famously brash American general, once said, "If everyone is thinking alike, then someone ain't thinking."

UNDERSTANDING THE DIFFERENT TYPES OF INNOVATION

1

The Purpose of the Chapter

The purpose of this chapter is to understand that innovation is a large tent, embracing many different types of innovation, and that you, as an innovator can work in any one of a variety of areas for your projects this semester.

Learning Objective

- Understand the different types of innovation, including product innovation, services innovation, and business model innovation.

We define innovation as creating and implementing ideas that create new customer value and/or ideas that improve and sustain the growth of organizations. Within this broad view of innovation, there are over a dozen specific types or categories of innovation. Innovations can be generally classified as either top-line or bottom-line initiatives. An example of a top-line innovation (revenue enhancer) would be a new product. An example of a bottom-line innovation (profit or margin enhancer) would be value engineering (pulling costs out of products or processes). Other examples of innovation are new channel innovation, branding innovation, customer experience innovation, platform innovation, and business model innovation. All of these innovations can be used in concert as a multi-prong or "innovation portfolio approach" to build, grow, and sustain an enterprise.

Over the past decade, innovation has been a major focus for most organizations, worldwide. In fact, in a recent survey of CEOs of publicly traded companies in the USA indicated that 72 percent of respondents said innovation was one of their top three priorities. Moreover, at the heart of every exciting startup is some type of exciting product or service innovation. Yet, research also reveals that sustained innovation remains one of the great challenges facing almost every company in America and that the average firm is failing at innovation most of the time. We believe the answer is to train people such as you in the concepts, methods, and applications of innovation – and then have you bring this thinking into established companies or startups. And that is why we have written this book.

It is also important to understand that within the creation of a new product, service, or system – particularly a technology intensive business – there is a balance between discovery of new technologies and the application of proven technologies to solve people's problems. It is easy to get confused by the difference between "invention" and "innovation." As an innovator, you must first understand these differences because your path toward success will likely be very different if you are focused on one or the other.

Invention is the discovery of new science and technology. For example, one of our former students led the team that developed a new flexible solar film that can be layered on top of radios, backpacks, vehicles, and so forth. A technology-intensive university spin-off—which is a company originating from a university research lab— typically takes years to realize its first dollar of true product revenue because there is so much research and development to do to get useful commercial products ready for market. Despite the great promise of his flexible solar film technology, this student knew he was in for a long haul. Not only did the "product" have to be perfected for specific applications, but the company had to design and develop an entirely new, capital-intensive manufacturing process for producing the flexible solar film. It was a very long haul. The company raised more than $100 million over a decade to commercialize this "power plastic" film—developing tremendous intellectual property along the way.But as a business, the venture could never provide sufficient return to investors for their $100 million because all the applications of the technology were small exploratory projects and programs. As impressive as the technology, the company as a business failed, and it's IP was purchased at a bargain basement price by a Chinese entity. "Invention" most often takes years, and for investors, the clock is always ticking. Perhaps with the exception of life sciences, the very front end of invention is typically best left to a well-funded university or corporate research labs.

Innovation, on the other hand, is the application of science and technology to solve problems for consumers, companies, governments, or society at large. Innovators, in particular, tend to apply their innovative thinking to find and address new market applications (e.g., new sets of emerging problems, new challenges, and new opportunities). For example, we see myriad mobile software development startups creating new applications—for mobile advertising, health monitoring, or smartphone-based financial transactions—based on existing communications standards or protocols. And they have access to published software development toolkits from Apple, Google (Android), Microsoft or open source that greatly expedite development time, as well as the time to first revenue dollar. For the innovator, the ability to use and deploy an existing set of hardware and software tools, chemicals, or any type of elemental ingredients is a very good thing.

Innovation is the foundation of a successful company or venture, and it also lies at the heart of successful educational and social services organizations. There are many types of innovation. Let's take a quick tour through the major types of innovation.

Product Innovation

From the customers' perspective, products are not purchased because of features. Products are purchased because they deliver a bundle of benefits or value to the customer. Keep this in mind when you are thinking about "product innovation." Many new products tend to fail because they do not deliver distinctive value or significant "points of difference." New products that tend to succeed deliver unique benefits to the user and do so better than competitive products. And, product innovation can come in different forms. We classify product innovation in three ways: incremental, dynamic, and discontinuous:

- Incremental product innovation occurs in a product category that already exists and where the customer is not required to learn new behaviors to use the product. For example, toothpaste manufacturers have introduced toothpaste that "whitens" teeth. This new dimension or innovation to the toothpaste does not require the user to learn new toothbrushing behavior. The bulk of product innovation in today's marketplace tends to be incremental innovation. This is sometimes referred to as a product line extension play. However, some companies are over-relying on this type of product innovation at their peril.

- Dynamic product innovation requires some changes in behavior on the part of the customer. For example, when a user switches from a manual toothbrush to an electric toothbrush he/she must learn how to use the new toothbrush properly and effectively. Toothbrushes as a category exist but the new electric toothbrushes are a new variation for the toothbrush category that requires customer learning and education. Dynamic product innovations can take longer to be adopted by customers and longer to diffuse across different customer groups over time because of this behavioral dimension.

- A discontinuous product innovation is "new-to-world" and creates a new product category. It also requires the customer to learn entirely new consumption behavior in order to use the product. Think about the first personal computer – it was a new-to-world concept that required customers to be educated about how to use it. Discontinuous product innovations are very rare and high risk to fully development. But, innovative companies that can commercialize discontinuous product innovations tend to be very successful.

Driving product innovation in established companies is the idea of finding adjacent market applications and repositioning current products to do new things. Every company, sooner or later, has to find new users to spur revenue growth. For example, Harley Davidson realized it was ignoring the female market. When it decided to reposition itself to appeal to female riders it doubled the number of potential customers for its motorcycles. Banks are working on new ways – including mobile apps – to reach Millennials.

Services Innovation

Services innovation is such an important component of our globalized economy. There is also a hierarchy of services innovation. Basic service improvements innovations are the most common type of new-service innovation. This involves modest changes in the performance of the current service, like serving customers quicker. Within this, style changes are the simplest type of new-service innovation and require no change in the service core or service process. Examples would be new uniforms for service personnel, new color schemes for the service facilities, or way scripts for employees to use when servicing customers. Service-line extensions innovations are additions to existing lines of services. For example, many banks now offer their customers insurance offerings. Supplementary-service innovations take the form of adding new elements to the core service or improving existing supplementary services that accompany the core service. FedEx Office, for example, offers high-speed Internet access at its locations for its customers. Lastly, there are disruptive services innovations are the introduction of new core concepts for markets that have not been previously defined. These include both new-service offerings and radical new processes. Fedex's introduction of overnight express delivery would be an example. Zipcar's hourly car rental business is another example of a disruptive services innovation.

Bundled Solutions Innovation

Bundled solutions innovation involves creating and delivering a single "package" as opposed to a customer having to search and pick and choose among different components that would make up a total solution. Bundled solutions deliver benefits to the customers because they do not have to make separate purchases and satisfaction is often enhanced given the overall solution is made available at the same time. A good example is in the vacation companies that offer a complete vacation package including airfare, hotel, car rental and activities. Think about what your customer buys besides your offerings and how they use those additional offerings in the context of using your offerings. There may be opportunities construct a bundled solution and/or to partner or co-brand with others that may be a part of a good bundled solution. The key is to find positive synergy between the components that make up the bundle. Moreover, it is possible that bundling may lower your marketing costs as well. However, be mindful that a bundle can be perceived by the customer as a "bargain" and thus the enterprise may have to engage in value-pricing of the bundle in that case. On the other hand, it is possible that the customer may value the bundled solution more than the individual items, separately. If so, the enterprise does not have to worry so much about bundled pricing.

Business Model Innovation

A business model is not a company's new products or services, per se, but how it makes money from its products or services. Within a business model is a) the revenue model, and b) an operational model. A revenue model includes how a company charges customers and the price it charges relative to competitors. The operational model defines the approaches and resources a company uses to produce that revenue. While many people might think that Uber is a services innovation, it more fundamentally a profound business model innovation, disrupting the traditional taxi business with a direct credit card account charging model, good discounts to regular taxi fares, a mobile app ride ordering channel, and people such as ourselves driving passengers in our own cars. Business model innovation is a much the essence of success for many new ventures as product or service innovation.

Process Innovation

Process innovation is when a company fundamentally improves the processes and procedures used to create and deliver value to customers. It can involve the implementation of a new production or delivery system as well as novel ways to deploy human capital to create new value customers. It is about finding ways to do things better, faster, cheaper or more conveniently for customers. Home health care is seeing profound process innovations in the delivery of health care to people in their homes. Financial services companies now have rapid approvals for consumer loans using automated risk management systems. Hopefully in your school the process of registering for classes or paying tuition bills has gone on-line and works reasonably well. Process innovation is an important area that innovators in established corporations think about every day.

Platform Innovation

Platform innovation is for engineers. It is the "under the hood" strategy for getting specific products and services developed and manufactured fast with high levels of profitability. A platform is a subsystem, module, or process that is used in more than one product, system or service. For example, a product platform might be an engine design used across many car models. In software, it might be a library of graphic interface objects shared across a word processor, a spreadsheet, a database and a charting program. A platform might also be a common process, such as an underwriting process used across multiple lines of property and casualty insurance. It takes innovative thinking to create platforms that can readily scale across different products, systems or services. But the payoff can be substantial. Just ask Honda, with its engines shared across cars and SUVs, or Microsoft with the common GUI and Cloud operating software across Office365, or UPS with its logistics systems and vehicles used across a variety of services.

Branding Innovation

It is often said, if an enterprise cannot or does not want to compete on price, it must win via brand innovation. Branding innovation is an activity in which the enterprise uses a name, phrase, design, symbols, or combination of these to identify its products and differentiate them from those of competitors. Good branding innovation leads to brand equity, the added value that a given brand name gives to a product beyond the functional benefits it provides. Brand equity provides a competitive advantage and allows the enterprise to charge a premium price for its brand. With branding innovation adhere to the old adage "be distinct or become extinct!" Importantly, an enterprise must determine if its brand(s) is still relevant and meaningful to your customer. If not, the enterprise will need to embark on a brand renovation strategy. Branding is about finding innovative ways to promote a company's brand, finding novel ways to reach customers with a compelling value proposition. Successful marketing innovation will typical include a compelling story, engagement with the customer and integration of traditional and new media. It focuses on making an emotional connection with the customer that is relevant and often delights the customer. Just think Apple with both its print, digital, and retail marketing initiatives that focus more on the user experience as on specific product features.

Channel Innovation

Channel innovation can come in many shapes and forms and the focus of the innovation can be technology-based, relational-based and/or structural-based. A technology-based channel innovation can involve deploying technology to streamline and enhance logistics, supply-chain and data exchange. It can result in e-procurement, e-sourcing and e-payment. Relational-based channel innovation can involve improving the relationships between members of the channel and/or the final customers particularly focusing on the buying process and customer care. Structural-based channel innovation includes multi-channel and cross-channel integration to improve market coverage, convenience to the customer while balancing costs to the enterprise. Novel structural-based channel innovations include D2C (direct-to-customer) channels and popup or flash retail concepts.

An innovator must consider all of these different types of innovations as s/he seeks to grow a business or other type of organization. Using largely working technologies allows the innovator to focus his or her innovation on solving a customer's problem, and then using specific methods to test if that customer truly represents a larger market upon which a great business can be built and sustained. Innovation becomes market-focused, using proven technologies and reliable methods for assessing demand and refining the business. This is essential for success. This holds equally true for corporate innovators reading this book. You want to be in the position of taking and deploying technology or basic science from your company to solve new problems, and from this, generate new revenue streams within a reasonable period of time. Try to find and integrate technologies that are ready to be integrated and applied to solve concrete, important customer problems. This way, you can keep your venture focused, fast, and effective.

Market-driven innovation demands that we answer basic questions about customers, buyers, and competitors before figuring out where we are going, and our business model for making money – or for some social enterprise – decide to not make money! To be effective with innovation, we need to understand the differences between customers and buyers (think of a retailer versus a consumer, or a procurement officer in a company versus an office worker). We also need to learn how to understand the problems, fears, and desires of these customers and buyers, so as to design distinctive, powerful products and service. And only then can we determine how we charge for things and our operating model as a company for R&D, manufacturing, sales, and service, e.g. the business model for the venture. Take all of points of learning together, and you will have the information and insight you need to design a new product, system, or service that is truly compelling to users – that brings a smile to their face in what the innovation does, how it performs, and how it used.

Each of the following chapters will present basic concepts and examples, and then a set of exercises to guide your research and advance your thinking. We want you to read these chapters and apply the exercises to your own projects before writing the formal business plan. In other words, we want you to perform the necessary in-market learning and thinking first before writing or presenting any "final" project. No shortcuts, please. Besides, if this homework becomes to the basis of a new product inside your company, or even the foundation for an entirely new venture, the work itself is going to be really interesting and lots of fun.

Now, we hope you are ready not only to work, but also to have fun in doing that work. Think of this as not just working for a grade, but working for yourself, for your own future. Creating something from scratch—seeing an innovation emerge from a team's creative thinking and focused application with users – is incredibly satisfying. Indeed, we hope that you become addicted to innovation and apply this type of creative yet structured thinking to everything you do for the rest of your lives!

DEFINING A CUSTOMER VALUE PROPOSITION IN THE CONTEXT OF AN INDUSTRY ECOSYSTEM

2

The Purpose of the Chapter

The purpose of this chapter is to develop an initial Customer Value Proposition for your innovation – a simple, powerful statement of the market focus and solutions focus in terms of the products and services you wish to create and sell. Then, we will learn how to place that Customer Value Proposition in the context of a dynamic, evolving ecosystem. Innovation takes place in a context. This chapter provides methods for establishing that innovation context. We also want you to use the methods in this chapter to screen different new innovation ideas in the class and to form teams built on an assessment of personal strengths and needs.

Learning Objectives

- Develop an initial Customer Value Proposition that we will continue to refine in the following chapters.

- Gather information on the attractiveness of a particular industry from a venture point of view, as well as to understand its key trends, competitors, and new venture activity, and sharpen the Customer Value Proposition.

- Map the industrial ecosystem that identifies the major stakeholders in your industry with which you can partner, or have to compete, as a startup or corporate venture. This sets the context for the venture idea, and helps to further sharpen the Customer Value Proposition.

- Screen the various Customer Value Propositions in the class to select the best ideas to pursue forward – hopefully yours!

Let's Get Started

You've come into the class for a reason: to learn how to design a new product, service, or for some you, a new business model for a product or service. Some of you might also be designing a new internal service or business process for within our own company or organization. Either way, the innovation needs to be distinctive from the customers' perspective. We bet you have ideas for a new innovation already. Let's get them down on paper in a structured way, and then learn how to vet them and select those with the most potential.

The structured method for putting down ideas is called the Customer Value Proposition. It is a simple, powerful way to express the target customer, the products or services to be provided to that customer, and the distinctive benefits for the customer from using your products or services. The clearer and more succinct the better.

Take a look at 2.1. It shows the major elements of a Customer Value Proposition:

- The name or brand of your products or services,

- The problem you wish to solve,

- The specific types of customers and specific use cases you wish to serve,

- The specific benefits you seek to provide, and

- How these benefits provide clear differentiation from current competitors.

This template can be applied to ideation for either a new product idea or a service. The example shown in Figure 2.1 is for a student venture that called its first product CoffeeBar. The problem the team sought to solve was "coffee on the go," where students or young professionals don't have time to wait in line at Starbucks. The specific use case in the Customer Value Proposition was as a replacement for morning coffee, in class or the office, or for studying later in the day. And the benefits were multiple: clean, Fair Trade coffee; excellent taste; a shot of caffeine; convenience and portability; and yes, nothing like it on the market at that time. It all fit together: brand name, problem solved, target customers and use case, core benefits, and competitive differentiation. The team proceeded to develop prototypes, test them with target users, find a certified outside manufacturer, and then raised enough money through KickStarter to launch its products into selected channels. Its sales doubled every month and within a year it was selling throughout the United States and a number of other countries around the world. But before all this success came the thinking: customer immersions leading to the development and refinement of a simple, bold Customer Value Proposition. It helped to guide the team during the startup process, providing focus, purpose, and design for the venture and its products.

You might have a software or system innovation idea in mind. Let's take the example of a graduate student innovation to create a Cloud-based system to monitor the elderly in their homes. A possible Customer Value Proposition for such a service might be:

Figure 2.1
The Customer Value Proposition Illustrated with CoffeeBar

ABC (give it a name) is our product / solution	CoffeeBar
That (solves what problem)	Coffee "on the go" for consumers who don't have the time to stop for a cup of coffee.
For (which target customers)	Busy students and working professionals, racing to class or to a meeting.
To be purchased by (which target buyers)	Premium, specialty retailers and direct to consumers through our own Website
The benefits we expect to provide (name the major benefits) will make ABC stand out from similar products and/or services.	All natural, vegan coffee in a no-mess, no spill single bar format, priced premium in the range of $3.00 a bar. A full cup of Fair Trade coffee in each bar
ABC is different than current (competitors/products) because of (why customers will buy it)	While the market for energy bars is crowded, there is no coffee bar on the market that is organic, Fair Trade.

Now, put it all together:

CoffeeBar is a coffee-infused energy bar delivering the boost you need without sacrificing nutrition. It is all natural, vegan, and made in the U.S. from a trusted manufacturer using Fair Trade sourced ingredients. Eat your coffee!

Elder Alert keeps a 24x7 electronic monitoring for the elderly living at home. Rather than rely on family member to make emergency calls, *Elder Alert* constantly monitors basic heart rate, movement, and other key factors through sensors woven into beds, couches and chairs to identify potential medical emergencies and automatically notify family member and first responders. Compared to current systems that require an elderly person to push a button, these systems work behind the scenes, day or night, and provide constant protection, particularly for someone living alone.

Remember, the Customer Value Proposition is a statement of customer focus and customer value as well as competitive distinctiveness. And it is done from the perspective of the target customer.

As another simple example, there may be some of you who wish to start some type of consulting or professional services firm. Let's use the example of a startup that builds mobile apps for large retailers seeking to use smartphones as a portal for their customer loyalty programs.

MobileApps is a consultancy that designs, develops, and helps retail clients deploy new mobile apps for customer loyalty programs. Once registered on the app, shoppers get news on promotions, receive digital coupons as valued customers, and can share their opinions about products. All major Smartphone platforms are supported. Information from the app is also provided to retailers to better inform marketing and merchandizing decisions. MobileApps is the new generation of smart retail customer loyalty technology.

Internal business processes can also use the Customer Value Proposition template to help focus the "better" in your innovative idea in contrast to an existing business process. That existing business process is "the competitor" and your customers are internal users. A lot of the work ticks on business process innovation. If this is your area of focus, don't just do a me-too process innovation; make it something special and value-rich for your internal users.

You might take a moment to use the open margins on the side of these pages to express that idea right now as your own Customer Value Proposition, first as the bullets in each section, and next, as a full statement. You will quickly see that the template will drive you to a clear, focused statement of purpose, benefit, and differentiation. Go for it!

Conducting a Rapid, Insightful Industry Analysis

Now that you are beginning to focus on a particular innovation idea, and getting more specific about its value for customers, it is time to get smart about the industry within which that idea sits.

The industry sets the context for any new venture. If the industry is growing rapidly, new products and services can readily find a home in the marketplace. If, on the other hand, the industry is besieged by low-cost producers cutting the bottom out of the market, any new innovation will have trouble making money unless someone redefines the traditional business model. Or, if an industry is mature, and highly stable in nature, it might be begging for disruption through a new business model, such as Airbnb or Uber. Therefore, before proceeding much further with in-depth customer research for an initial Customer Value Proposition, it is first very important to understand the industry in which the innovation will find a home as the basis of a startup or corporate venture, or as a product line or brand innovation. And, there are good methods for conducting a rapid, insightful industry analysis. We want to do this as quickly and effectively as possible, searching the Web for important information.

There are two important points before we learn methods for industry analysis. First, it often does not make sense to innovate in a flat or declining industry as defined by the growth of sales, or lack thereof, by companies participating in that industry. You need to work in an industry that has users – consumers or businesses -- who are spending money on solutions like yours. And even in a given industry, certain segments or parts might be growing really fast, while others are growing slowly or not at all. Take the solar industry. The industry for the design and manufacture of photovoltaic cells transformed from a high growth area at the turn of the Millennium to a tough, slow growing one due to oversupply and price dumping by offshore manufacturers. At the same time, the segment for installing and servicing solar energy systems has continued to grow at a healthy rate, partly fueled by government subsidies, but also by consumer demand in the face of rising energy prices and consumer-friendly energy purchase business models.

This leads to the second idea: successful innovators typically find a rapidly growing niche within a larger industry. The innovation team concentrates on that specific group of customers and applications, develops strength over five years, and becomes a market leader in that niche – and then expands into adjacent niches, either through internal growth or through acquisitions. The bottom line: successful innovators target hot niches within robust markets. Industry analysis helps identify these hot niches.

Now, let's turn to a set of specific methods.

Identifying the Segments and Niches Within Larger Industries

An **industry** is a group of firms that produce products or services that are close substitutes for one another, and that serve the same general set of customers. Most industries can be subdivided into specific **segments** that include a set of competitors that address particular customer groups. For example, the financial services industry includes many segments: investment banking, commercial and retail banking, insurance, money management, and so forth.

Often, the segments of an industry also have sub-segments, or niches, that include their own sets of customers, competitors, and commercial offerings. For example, in the insurance industry alone there are property and casualty, life, health, pet health insurance, and long-term care niches.

Some segments/niches may have low growth, low profitability (over the past several years, for example, the property and casualty industry is suffering high claims due to natural catastrophes, storms, and the like), and little innovation; others, such as long-term care insurance or home healthcare, may exhibit dynamic growth and an abundance of opportunities to make money. The central idea here is for you, the innovator, to do your research to focus not only on a promising industry, but to find the segment, and the niche within that segment, that offers you the best chances of starting a company and growing it to be a leader in that niche. Often, a niche that is emerging and seems small has a way of growing rapidly and becoming a major market in its own right.

Competition is an important consideration. Why take on Apple or Google directly in one of their chosen target customer and use case situations? Think of a different customer or a different use case, build a great company, and then perhaps one of these giants will want to acquire it as part of its own growth strategy. For example, one of our students started a company called CloudLock. Its Customer Value Proposition is to provide a secure virtual private network for corporations using Google Docs (instead of Microsoft Office or 360). Gil, the founder, decided not to take on Google directly but to complement it with a value-added service. Gil's company is growing by leaps and bounds, and no doubt someday a large technology company, or Google itself, will acquire it.

Like Gil, as an innovator you should not try to take on an entire industry and all of its established players. Define your target market in such a way that your innovation is like a rifle shot aimed at a specific opportunity, with just a handful of competitors or perhaps a larger number of tiny competitors. This approach leads you to find a particular niche within the larger industry, to strive to become the leading player in that niche, and to expand from there. This lends focus to the new enterprise, and focus is all-important for everything else you will do: what to make, how to produce, how to sell and promote, and whom to hire.

It is all the better if your industry analysis steers you to a segment/niche that exhibits a healthy rate of growth in terms of current or expected sales. We call this strong customer demand. It is also good if there is a clear distribution channel to reach those customers, be it the Web, a major retailer, or an industrial partner. Otherwise, building an entirely new channel to market typically requires millions of dollars, if not tens of millions of dollars.

Therefore, you need to understand an industry both in broad strokes as well as what is happening in its various major segments and particularly interesting niches within those segments. At the end of the day, you are going to select one of those niches to —one that matches up with your work experience, education, personal connections, and professional passions.

As you study a particular industry, its segments, and niches, look for positive indicators in the following areas:

- The current size and growth rates of customer demand, e.g., sales, in your target industry, and even better, your target segment or more specifically, niche

- Favorable major customer and consumer trends sweeping across the industry

- Fragmented competition or a manageable level of competitive intensity

- The presence of winners in your target industry, showing that money is there to be made

- A strong level of startups, VC investment, and M&A activity

- Positive technology trends based on some significant breakthroughs and innovations (such as mobile, analytics, sustainable systems, etc.)

- Strong channels to reach customers with newer, better products or services

- No major barriers to entry for new firms in terms of the amount of capital needed for a startup, a lockup of key suppliers, or impossible to crack distribution channels

The very first step is to go onto your favorite search engine and begin to type in key words with descriptors for each of the eight bullet points above, including a label for your industry target, such as "energy bar market," "Fair Trade coffee industry," or, "sales home healthcare," "venture capital home healthcare," and "new trends technology home healthcare." Sit back and watch a wealth of information unfold before your eyes. Start browsing through the links.

When an interesting industry trade report or company is mentioned, explore. If it is a report, see if you can get a copy of it or an article with industry data for free. Look for industry reports from trade associations, articles that size a particular industry or emerging segment or niche, or a new product announcement by a company, large or small. You are looking for facts, figures, potential customers, channel partners, and competitors. If it is a company, go to its Website, look at the management team, the Board (who will be investors if it is a startup), the products, and the customers. If the company is publicly traded, take a look at the financial statements to see who is making money in the industry, and *how they are making it.*

Create a set of folders on your computer desktop and store this information for later use. Most important, begin to organize this information into overall industry information and more specific segment or niche information. You will be surprised just how much information exists, *for free*, on the Web for innovators willing to do a little homework.

Be thorough investigating these areas. The result should point the way to the robust business opportunity you need to start a successful company. In fact, if you have the passion, it will be hard to pull yourself away from the computer: there will be too much information! However, after a couple of hours at the keyboard, sit back and begin to craft a story in your mind about the most attractive part of the industry you wish to enter. This will later become the **industry analysis** section of your business plan and investor pitch. Now, let's dig a little bit more into methods for industry analysis.

Understanding Industry Structure, Current Size, and Growth Rates

As noted above, industries tend to be comprised of multiple segments. Each segment contains different types of customers and different uses for products and services. Some of these segments might have low growth and low profitability; others might have dynamic growth and lots of opportunities to make money. This reasoning also extends to the niches within major industry segments. Understanding an industry structure is essential for developing an industry focus, and from that, a compelling plan.

Current size and growth rates for major segments/niches are critically important. Developing a new product, service, or business model innovation a flat or declining segment is also usually a waste of time. Look for areas where robust growth is anticipated for years to come. As the saying goes, "A rising tide lifts all boats."

TIP: Using Government Data Sources to Size Industries, Segments, and Niches

While it is often possible to find reports on the Web that present current industry size and projected growth rates—and from these, to create an industry structure—sometimes you need to go to the source data behind these reports. Certain regions in the world maintain excellent databases for sizing industries. For example, there are the North American Industry Classification System (NAICS) and U.S. Census Bureau data (www.census.gov/eos/www/naics and http://census.gov/econ/census07). NAICS provides common industry definitions for the United States, Canada, and Mexico, and groups the economic activities of specific companies into specific industries and their major segments. Similar classification systems exist in Europe, Japan, and the BRIC countries (Brazil, Russia, India, and China).

Let's say you want to start an organic, hydroponic vegetable growing business that would locate greenhouses on the rooftops of large, urban retail stores and reuse the heat and water from these stores for climate control in the greenhouses themselves. Using NAICS, you would find the "industry" defined as "Sector 11"—called Agricultural, Forestry, Fishing, and Hunting. Then, you would drill down to Crop Production—"Subsector 111." In doing so, you have refined your industry space to a specific segment. Here, you can examine market size and growth across a range of crops. But, given that you intend to operate in the "greenhouse" space, you should define and identify your target more narrowly—a classic example of focusing in on a "niche." We do this by looking at "Subsector 1114"—labeled Greenhouse, Nursery, and Floriculture Production—that provides more specific insight regarding the size and growth of that niche. But wait! It is even possible to drill further, to Subsector 11141—Food Crops Grown Under Cover (exactly what you will be doing). It is possible to drill down to another level—Subsector 111419—and examine data on specific crops grown under cover. Using these data, you discover that organic tomatoes are in greater demand and selling at significantly higher margins than mushrooms! These industry data will help you to properly plan your product offerings.

Understand the Major Customer/Consumer Trends Sweeping Across an Industry

The point here is to make sure that your customer value proposition will be addressing a major customer need and/or be taking advantage of an important new technological capability transforming an industry and the various players operating within it.

Most industries are in flux, driven by the combination of technological innovation and larger societal trends and challenges. This creates new possibilities for innovators and threatens existing incumbent firms competing with yesterday's products, services, and business models. In this part of your industry analysis, you need to understand the major trends affecting customers and competitors in your target industry.

Here are a few examples to consider:

- **The security industry:** September 11th created a new segment called homeland security. A host of startups and large defense contractors have been innovating with systems that feature smart software using new, tiny sensors to gather real-time information in the effort to stop terrorists. This continues to be a robust market[1].

* **The healthcare industry:** The aging of the population, as well as new government regulations, have created growth opportunities in a range of segments: cost control in hospital-based care; new monitoring technologies for home healthcare; and new types of drugs based on technologies such as DNA sequencing, proteomics, and the like. Personalization of therapies is said to be the future of healthcare.

* **Energy:** The cost of fossil fuels is driving change across multiple industries, be it solar/wind power, materials for home construction, transportation, and the distribution of electricity itself—all the way down to our refrigerators!

* **Industrial equipment and transportation:** Companies increasingly want greater efficiency in the operation of equipment as well as higher levels of automation, safety, and machine uptime. Machine-to-machine diagnostics, communications, and repair is transforming major classes of industrial and transportation equipment. Some refer to this as M2M. Others as IoT or the Internet of Things. Sensors are placed on or in equipment to monitor machine health. Any problems are communicated – typically through a wireless network – to a central server where algorithms get a fix on the specific problem and recommend corrections. Computer companies use this for remote diagnostics; Caterpillar constantly monitors its tractors from afar; and military equipment of all sorts also has automated M2M sensing, diagnostics, and repair.

* **Climate change, water utilization, and smarter energy consumption:** Putting politics aside, diversity of energy supply and more intelligence in consumption are bound to be major drivers for innovation and new ventures in the future. Estimates are that a third of the water pipes underground in cities are leaking! How might you detect leaks, monitor piping, and make money by doing so? Or, the development of cogeneration systems for both commercial and home applications?

* **Government regulations for specific industries:** Government regulation can drive entrepreneurial opportunities. For example, in financial services, fraudulent company accounting led to the Sarbanes-Oxley legislation put into effect in 2002 in the United States, and to a host of new software and service ventures to help companies become compliant.

If your customer value proposition – either in the need it addresses or in the solution you propose – can fit within an industry transformation such as those described above, your innovation will be all the more exciting to both customers and investors. No sense in creating a pedestrian, "me-too" proposition, where all you can do is compete on lower price.

---

1 Meyer, M. H., and Poza, H. (2009). Venturing adjacent to the core: From defense to homeland security. Research Technology Management, (May): 31–48.

TIP: Using Trade Association Data to Get a Handle on Industry Size, Segments, and Growth Rates

Trade associations and other related nonprofit groups often gather activity-related information from their respective members and make these data available to the public. This can be a great source of data on industry size, industry segments, growth rates, and major trends. These data are often updated on a regular basis, so the information is current.

There are literally thousands of different trade associations, not just in the United States but also around the globe. You can see if there is a trade group for your target industry by simply doing a Web search for "trade association [industry name]." Or your university library might have a copy of the Encyclopedia of Associations, which contains information on more than 150,000 specific trade associations, both in the United States and abroad. From these searches, you can then go to the association's Website and search for freely available information.

Figure 2.2 shows an example. It comes from an industry trade group, the U.S. Travel Association (www.ustravel.org). After taking a look at the data in the figure, visit the association's Website and look under the "Research" menu to see specific forecasts for domestic and international travel, as well as the number of trips for business and leisure travelers. Another Website maintained by the U.S. Travel Association, poweroftravel.org, provides more information, such as the fact sheet shown in Figure 2.2. You will also see that nearly all association Websites have reports both for the public and for members.

There are also many industry research consulting firms that gather similar types of data and pride themselves on being experts in predicting industry trends. Your business library just might have access to some of these research firms' publications. One of the best in this regard is Frost & Sullivan. Some business research libraries have Frost & Sullivan reports on their shelves. However, be prepared to see a price for such reports in the hundreds of dollars, if not more. This, or joining a trade association, might be an investment you have to make to gather the data you need to raise substantial amounts of capital from professional investors. For now, however, look for industry data on the Web, or ask friends who might already have access to such data. Without the numbers, it will be hard to objectively assess industry appeal in terms of size, growth, and the most attractive segments for starting a new venture.

Data such as these will prove to be very useful later on when you are writing the Industry Analysis section of your business plan (not until Chapter 11!). So, whatever data you gather, remember to place them in an electronic or physical folder, clearly marked for later use.

There are often news stories on these major trends, new product announcements, and customer applications that can give you a sense of change and innovation. Each region of the world has its own information sources—so search them out on the Web and use them!

Competition and the Existence of Successful Business Models

The Overall Competitive Intensity in an Industry

Some industries have one or two large leaders and half a dozen second-tier competitors, all jockeying for incremental gains in market share by introducing a new product or service and, just as often, lowering prices. It's very tough for a startup to compete in such an environment. A new corporate venture, on the other hand, stands a better chance because it can often leverage the corporation's brands, distribution channels, manufacturing, and credibility to break into the market with a new solution. And if you are working in an established company with a well-known product line or services, innovating in this space is probably not a good but necessary thing.

At the same time, most innovators avoid areas of intense, concentrated competition and seek out **fragmented markets** in which there are many small competitors and no dominant leaders. In fragmented markets, an innovator with an attractive value proposition, a strong work ethic, adequate capital, and imagination has a fair shot at success. Even big companies look for new adjacent markets with less competition as a focus for product and service innovation to grow revenue.

Be a User, Yourself

Go see how current products or services akin to your innovation are used by consumers or companies. Begin to watch others use the product or service. If you can, try using the product or service yourself. This is often how innovators invent "a

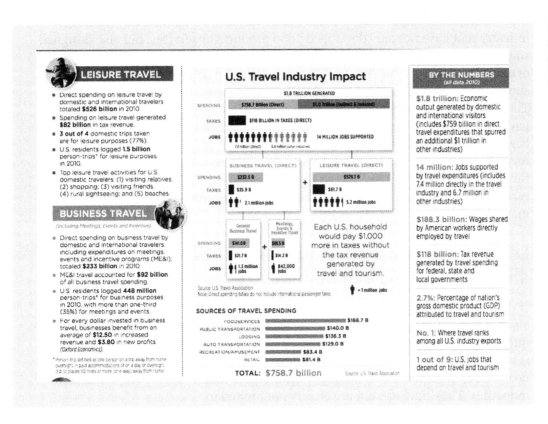

Figure 2.2
An Example of Trade Association Industry Information: The U.S. Travel Association

better mousetrap." If you are doing a service innovation, say at your own school, be a customer for that service and take careful note of the flaws, inefficiencies, and frustrations that you encounter. These will be the sources of your own innovation. The innovator differentiates by solving problems in that use case in a way that is different, more special, and more pleasing than existing solutions in the market. In later chapters, we will learn methods on how to approach this. It is so much fun and so satisfying to bring a smile to the user's face once he or she turns on the ignition!

Next, think about the place of purchase. If you are developing a consumer product that sits on a retail shelf, visit some retail stores soon after class. See the major competitors already sitting on the shelf. Pretend to be a customer for a moment: see how competitors' products sit on shelf. Ask them why they recommend a particular product over another? Is it a certain set of features? Or, do you surmise that they are receiving a larger sales commission for one product over the next, or that their store makes more money selling one particular brand over another. From all this, you want to know how a market leader competes in the *place of purchase.*

The Presence of Winners in an Industry: Study Them!

As you study an industry and its various segments, you should take note of companies that achieved success in your specific industry segment or niche. Look at the products or services they provided, how they sold these into market, how they charged for things, and their recipe for making money. If there are no winners in your target industry, don't assume you are that much smarter than anyone else. It might be a poor industry in which to start a company – and you might have to pivot to a new innovation idea.

Also— and just as important—are there relatively new companies in your target industry that have not only developed good products or services, but also designed ways to make money—business models—that seem to be scaling to the point of achieving considerable success? These models of past success and emerging success are so very important to understand as you design your own business. They will also tell you which parts of your target industry are generating profits for participants. Take note of these companies and read all you can about them. Then begin to consider the best way for your innovation to proceed and to make money. As part of this, also keep an eye out for areas in an industry understand that are the subjects of venture investment or corporate investment activity. Innovation rarely takes place in a vacuum. See what others entrepreneurs are doing in your market space.

Learn About the Major Technology Trends and Breakthroughs in an Industry

If your venture is going to be technology intensive, there is no sense in not riding a major technology trend and/or exploiting a technology breakthrough created at university or company. Ride that wave to success – *as long as the breakthrough is sufficiently stable* as the basis of building a real solution. Fortunately, there is no shortage of important technology trends and breakthroughs sweeping across industries. These include, but are clearly not limited to:

- Mobile Technologies, for just about everything – finance, health, retail, entertainment, etc.

- Cloud Technologies – for the delivery of so many services, and also providing the opportunity to implement a subscription model for products such as software and eliminate copying.

- Analytics and Database Technologies – to drive the smarter healthcare, supply chains, retail, and transportation. Personalization of medicine is also a new frontier.

- Web and Mobile Powered Social Media – which is increasingly important for even the most traditional of industries, such as personal banking and finance.

- Security Technologies – including tremendous advances integrating video with databases for surveillance, threat detection, and alerting.

- Nanomaterials – materials are becoming smarter, more durable, and multifunctional. An example would be a shoulder pad that expands upon contact to provide more protection.

- Real-time Sensing Technologies – the Internet of Things is sweeping across industrial, healthcare, and consumer industries.

- Personalized Medicine – this is a synthesis of gathering real time information about individual patients through sensors and more traditional blood work, etc. to specifically direct treatment, both highly specific drug formulations, targeting agents, and treatment protocols. (Yes, it's complicated, but this is where the future of medicine is heading.)

- Incorporating a major technology trend or breakthrough into a new venture makes the company all the more interesting to customers and investors. It is a branding phenomenon as much as it is a new technology. However, be careful. In most cases involving professional investors, you need to develop new products and services and get to at least a proof of concept if not first dollar of sales within nine to eighteen months. Medical devices might be longer in time cycle, new drugs even longer. In general, except for the life sciences, investors have little patience for funding the development of a technology breakthrough that itself will take three or four years in R&D before actual product development and application can begin.

Understand the Channels of Distribution Within an Industry

The innovator seeks strong, clear channels of distribution that are receptive to new product or service innovations. For example, the third-party software business development programs of Microsoft, IBM, Oracle, and others provide a path to their respective customers. Or, if you are doing a consumer products innovation, understanding the willingness of premium specialty retailers to try new products such as yours is very important. Whole Foods Market, Petco, and Target are all good examples. If you are doing a life sciences innovation, today large pharmaceutical companies are desperate to fill their depleting pipelines with new potential drugs. Each one of these represents channels as well as development partners. New, small firms can prosper by aligning themselves with larger corporations that have access to large markets.

You need to make sure that the supply of necessary components, technologies, or ingredients needed for your types of products or services are readily available and reasonably priced. For a food company, that means recipe ingredients. If you are thinking of manufacturing solar energy panels, you should check the availability of key inputs, such as silicon. For a software company, these are the necessary software development tools. For a services company, that means reasonably priced labor that can be trained up to standard, and then low-cost yet powerful information technology to support the services.

On the same note, how eager are suppliers of key materials to deal with startups such as yours? You may find, for example, that a major competitor has "locked up" those suppliers. You have to be proactive and actually ask whether or not suppliers are open to cooperate with you. Suppliers will be honest if you ask, but it is your responsibility to determine this situation.

Try to Assess If There are Barriers to Entry in an Industry: Capital Needed, Supply, or Channel

A thorough investigation of a target industry must also consider the presence of barriers to entry. A barrier to entry is a de facto force that prevents a new entrant from scaling up an innovation either as a new business or part of an existing business. A barrier to entry is any requirement—capital, technical know-how, and so on—that makes industry or market entry difficult or impossible. Of the many barriers faced by industry outsiders, three are particularly important for innovators: capital and time, manufacturing, and marketing.

- **Capital and Time Barriers:** Entry to some industry segments/niches requires huge amounts of capital—amounts that few entrepreneurs can raise. In others, years of R&D are needed to develop marketable products. As you can imagine, these two barriers usually go hand in hand. Consider, for example, the pharmaceutical industry, where more than ten years and close to a billion dollars are typically needed from start to launch for a single new drug! On the other hand, Web-based social networking presents minimal time and small amounts of investment capital to get started. Launching a new Web-based business can be fast and inexpensive.

- **Supply Barriers:** This is often part of manufacturing. Access to certain types of manufacturing at a required price level can be difficult. Or, a large competitor may have monopolized access to certain vital raw materials. Fortunately, these days there are great options for finding co-manufacturers and gaining access to raw materials and componentry, not the least of which are Alibaba if your venture needs to purchase materials, or Amazon Web Services if you require lots of computing power.

• **Distribution/Channel Barriers:** Marketing is the third major barrier to entry that an entrepreneur needs to consider. Gaining access to large retailers can be difficult and costly. For example, a new food venture faces a serious financial obstacle if it needs to pay "slotting fees" to national groceries in order to get its products on the shelves. Slotting fees can reach to several million dollars or more. Whole Foods Market, on the other hand, does not charge slotting fees, nor do "club" channels such as Costco. It is no surprise that food entrepreneurs go to specialty retailers and club stores to avoid this huge upfront expense. And, the Web is the great liberator for developing an eCommerce capability alongside more traditional channel selling.

After doing your industry research, you can bring the industry analysis together by doing your best to complete the template shown in Figure 2.3. We call it the Industry Analysis Scorecard. You are looking for positive facts, trends, and stories that point to the industry being a good one for a startup. Take a look at the template now – you will be gathering data to complete the template later in the Reader Exercises at the end of this Chapter. The Scorecard contains all the major elements we just described for industry analysis in a single, convenient assessment form.

How are competitors' products merchandized? Are any sitting at the preferred eye level? Does the packaging stand out? Or, if an individual sells your product or service, simply find a salesperson in the store or dealership and see how that individual tries to sell you. Is a competitor's product or service high priced and full featured, or low-priced without as many features, or somewhere in the middle? Where do you want your solutions to sit in terms of price-performance? And, think about how you want your new products or services to be represented in a way that is special and differentiated from current competitors – and bring these insights into your planning.

Often overlooked is the importance of understanding competitors' channel strengths and promotional strategies. Please do not be only product or technology-focused. In addition to having innovative, best-of-breed products or services, you need to strive for excellence in channel. Great companies have both: Apple, IBM, Amazon, and Google—they truly excel on both fronts.

Next, with industry and competitive analysis in hand, you then need to complete this scoping activity by getting a handle on the full industry ecosystem. Who are the key players in different parts of that ecosystem? Where is the research being performed or the tools developed that your innovation will use? Who is funding innovations like yours? Who are the major suppliers or manufacturers that your innovation might use? And, what are the primary channels to market for your innovation? These are fundamental questions that you need to understand at a basic level and integrate into one, powerful and guiding picture. To do this, we like to use an industry ecosystem map. It is shown in Figure 2.4.

First, the structure of the ecosystem map. On the top or vertical axis is the logical value chain for providing value to the customer. We start at technology discovery,

Figure 2.3
The Industry Analysis
Scorecard

	Facts/Data About Your Target Industry (Bullet points facts)	Industry Score (1-10)
Target industry/segment niche size and growth rate		
Favorable trends sweeping across industry		
Competitive intensity: fragmented competition		
The presence of winners		
High level of startups and M&A activity		
Positive technology trends based on some significant break-throughs and innovations		
Strong channels to reach customers		
No major barriers to entry in terms of capital needed, supply channels, and distribution		
	Total Score	

Scoring Key: 1 to 10, where:
    1 is "a potential show-stopper for a new venture", 3 is "a significant chal
    lenge", 5 is "neither a barrier nor supporting success", 7 is "conducive to a
    new venture", and 10 is "an ideal setup for venture success"

proceed to materials supply, next to actual product or service development and commercialization, and then to distribution of the products or services. And then, customers – whoever they may be within an industry – typically require some type of service or support. If you are clever as an innovator, you will figure out how to minimize support requirements or, build customer support into your business model as a money making service and/or the opportunity to upsell existing customers.

The vertical axis on the left side represents the logical players in an industry eco-system. These include the discoverers of new technologies, investors in startups,

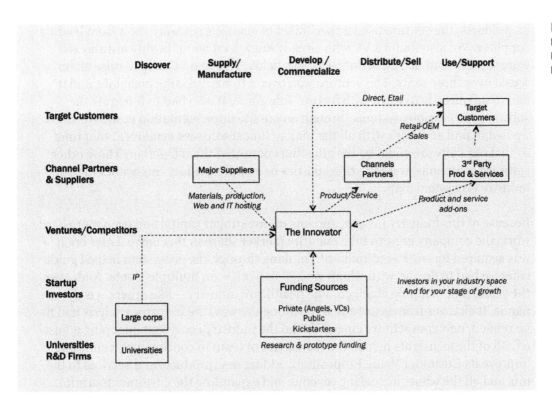

Figure 2.4
Map the Innovation
Ecosystem: Know the
Essential Players

innovating companies or nonprofits, channel and supply partners, and then the customers themselves.

The two axes in the template – different types of key players and the value chain of product or service creation and delivery – create a framework upon which you can identify the major actors necessary for a particular innovation idea, and the relationships you would like to have with them. You can use arrows and labels to be even more specific about the flow of goods and services, and write in specific names of key suppliers, channel partners, and even those investors or other sources of funding that would be best for financing your type of innovation because of their prior track records.

Each actor in the ecosystem map is specific to your target industry, segment, or niche. For example, in the CoffeeBar example, there are specific suppliers and qualified manufacturers for healthy, Fair Trade ingredients and food manufacturing, just as there are certain channels where an all natural, Vegan product is best sold, including Whole Foods or Sprouts.

Or, let's consider a software example. One of your authors helped start a company where the Customer Value Proposition was to create a secure mechanism for physicians and nurses to log onto clinical systems in the hospital. The team wanted to have the patient records across clinical systems synchronized so that people with similar sounding names don't get one another's diagnoses and drugs! It was (and remains) a big problem for lots of hospitals around the world. Achieving this synchronization provides huge benefits for doctors and nurses, as well as keeping patients safe inside hospitals. At the time when the company was started, there were only two direct competitors, but none truly focused on healthcare. To develop its products, the venture used a specific set of enabling software tools from leading suppliers. We also found a VC who already knew a lot about healthcare and software security and had a portfolio in these fields. This one VC helped raise about $30M over three years. The venture won over a thousand large hospitals, and it had to sell directly to them with its own salesforce. It also had to integrate the software with various systems through an on-site implementation crew. We knew we had to find and work with all the major clinical software vendors at that time so that our software could be the glue that connected them together. These other software companies were the third parties or complementary innovators in the industry ecosystem map.

Because of this industry insight, and lots of investment capital and even more hard work, the company grew to take majority market share in this niche. Later on, it was acquired for over $150 million! Thinking through the ecosystem helped guide what we had to do and with whom we had to work – on multiple fronts. And, over the years, that mapping changed. The healthcare industry – like others – is dynamic. It changes from year to year. So along the way, the industry analysis had to be refined, new competitors emerged, and the industry ecosystem mapping adjusted. All of these insights helped the management team to continuously refine and improve its Customer Value Proposition, adding new products and services to the mix and all the while, increasing revenue and expanding the customer footprint.

You can do the same thing for your innovation idea. It is simply a matter of having the methods and discipline to do industry and competitive analysis right up front, mapping your industry ecosystem, and keep on doing these things as your innovation grows.

READER EXERCISES

Now it is your turn to apply these frameworks to your own venture ideas: Customer Value Propositions, Industry Analysis, Direct Competitor Analysis, and Ecosystem Mapping.

Before getting started, lets share some thoughts about student project teams as opposed to solo efforts. The work for this course is often performed in teams to emulate the venture team startup process. But we all know the pitfalls of projects teams in a course such as this. Most people will work really hard, but there always seems to be the one or two people who slack off and fail to add real value. If you do recruit team members for a project, have a separate discussion offline in terms of roles and responsibilities. Define the work, week by week, and have an agreement on mutual obligations. Do this early in the project so that everyone understands the "skin in the game" that each team member needs to contribute. Then, have a process for reviewing each other's work. And seek counsel from your professor if the situation persists. These methods are valuable, but require real commitment and work. You don't want to have people join your team just because they think your idea is "cool." They've got to be willing to work. As an entrepreneur, you don't have the time, nor should you have the patience, to carry noncontributors on your back. Now on to the assignments for this chapter.

Step 1: Develop a Customer Value Proposition for Your Venture Idea

Take a look at Figure 2.5, the Customer Value Proposition Template. We assume that you came into this class with several ideas for a new venture. Start working through the template with one of these ideas. Start at the top and work your way to the bottom. Try to write a complete statement at the bottom. Then, do it for a second idea, or even better, share your work with a few other classmates. Who has the sharpest, clearest Customer Value Proposition? Who has the best understanding of the customer use case? If you had to bet your own money (or for this semester, your time), which Customer Value Proposition would you choose?

As teachers we love to see two or three students collaborate on a new venture idea. The template gives a focus to your conversations, fostering not just creativity, but real synergy. And you will soon see if your team has the real makings of a team. If someone doesn't have any inputs to a venture idea, encourage them to do so, and if they still don't have any inputs, perhaps they need to find another team. In developing a new venture, everyone really needs to roll up their sleeves, think, and work.

Step 2: Conduct an Industry Analysis

Once you have settled on a Customer Value Proposition that appears to have the most promise as the basis for a new innovation, it is then time to perform an industry analysis for that idea.

This is a very important exercise. You need to search the Web and other data sources for information regarding your target industry: trade association reports, news stories, etc. Cast a broad net. Find technology changes, channel changes, and competitors entering your industry. Look for recent venture investment and M&A activity in your industry. You also need to search sources such as MoneyTree Report (www.pwcmoneytree.com) to see the current flow of angel and venture financing into that sector. Examples of industries might

Figure 2.5
The Customer Value
Proposition Template

One or two bullet points each

ABC (give it a name) is our product / solution	
That (solves what problem)	
For (which target customers)	
To be purchased by (which target buyers)	
The benefits we expect to provide (name the major benefits) will make ABC stand out from similar products and/or services.	
ABC is different than current (competitors/ products) because of (why customers will buy it)	
Now, put it all together:	

be biotechnology, software, medical devices, energy, media and entertainment, networking and equipment, or healthcare services.

Then, once you have gathered these data, we want you to score the attractiveness of each dimension in Figure 2.6 for your industry target. We have provided nine important dimensions for you to consider. Next, make an honest assessment of these dimensions, using data where possible. Is the segment/niche a good place to innovate? Does it have favorable industry dynamics or not?

The highest possible score is 80. An industry scoring over 60 in this template is truly worth consideration as a venue for an innovation. Any industry scoring below 40 should probably be avoided. If your industry scores in the midrange on the scale—say, 40 to 50 —then you must think about how you will overcome industry problems and obstacles.
If the assessment score is low, you might wish to consider looking at a different industry or a different segment of the industry. Otherwise, you need to have a serious discussion about how to overcome the negative dynamics you have uncovered. When it comes time to raise money from professional investors, assume that they know the potholes just as well as anyone else. Seasoned professionals are good at uncovering "show stoppers," defined as industry dynamics that make even a well-managed innovation hard to grow.

Fortunately, you should have more than one Customer Value Proposition around which to perform an industry analysis. If your industry assessment comes up negative, select the next best idea, and take a run at it. Industry analysis needs to be fast and effective. An initial, concentrated two or three-hour effort will tell you a lot about most industries. If you are working as a team, have each team member explore a different Customer Value

	Facts/Data About Your Target Industry (Bullet points facts)	Industry Score (1-10)
Target industry/segment niche size and growth rate		
Favorable trends sweeping across industry		
Competitive intensity: fragmented competition		
The presence of winners		
High level of startups and M&A activity		
Positive technology trends based on some significant break-throughs and innovations		
Strong channels to reach customers		
No major barriers to entry in terms of capital needed, supply channels, and distribution		
	Total Score	

Figure 2.6
The Industry Dynamics Scorecard

Scoring Key: 1 to 10, where:
   1 is "a potential show-stopper for a new venture", 3 is "a significant challenge",
   5 is "neither a barrier nor supporting success", 7 is "conducive to a new
   venture", and 10 is "an ideal setup for venture success"

Proposition and then reconvene to make collective decisions based on the facts presented. Passion is important – but do not mistake it for facts. You want to innovate in a promising industry based on real facts about industry growth, real technology trends, and real opportunities to better serve current and emerging customers in that industry.

Step 3: Develop an Industry Ecosystem Map

Figure 2.7 is the Ecosystem Template. From your industry analysis, you should have many of the players already identified. But take the time to reach further. Where is the basic re-

Figure 2.7
Industry
Ecosystem
Template

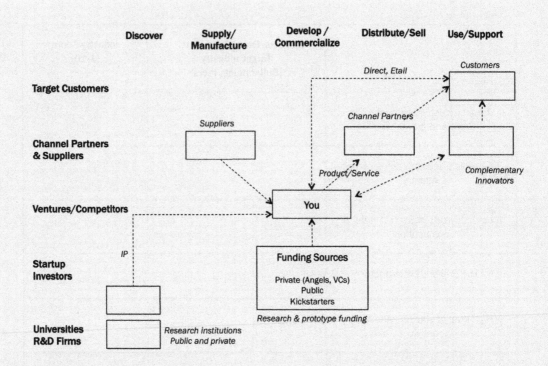

search being formed (if that matters to your innovation)? Who are the important suppliers and contract research organizations or manufacturers with whom you can partner for your business? If you were a customer for your own product or service, what would be the single best way or channel through which to purchase and get support for it? And importantly, as customers tend to use an array of products or services together from different companies, who are the complementary innovators that you need to know about, and later on, contact and develop partnerships?

Developing a rich industry ecosystem map provides the insight you need to position an innovation as an exciting entrant into your target industry. You want your innovation to be "hot" within your industry, to in some way connect and serve as a focus point for where the industry is heading. Who are the funding sources that should be interested in your vision? Think broadly. It might be a government sources for R&D to commercialize university technology, an active angel group in your region known for doing deals in your space, or a VC whose Website clearly shows through the focus and scope of their investment portfolio that your vision could be part of their vision.

Developing an initial ecosystem map should itself be an hour or two of concentrated activity. Hand draw your map before spending the time to put it into PowerPoint. New players within the map will invariably emerge through the course of the semester and you can keep fine-tuning it as the weeks proceed.

As a last step, prepare your templates to be shared with others inside and outside of class. You will find these simple forms a great way to solicit feedback, learn more, and perhaps a way to build your own innovation team and extended support network. Certain individuals will get very excited about your thinking and engage with a certain intensity around your templates. Those are the people you want.

FOCUSING IN ON THE TARGET CUSTOMER:
User and Buyers

3

The Purpose of the Chapter

The previous chapter helped you determine the focus for your innovation by defining a customer value proposition in the context of your industry and direct competitors. We will be refining your customer value proposition throughout the innovation process in the next five chapters, all culminating in a Reality Check that will test not just the customer value proposition, but your product strategy, business model, and branding strategy. This is fundamentally important and exciting stuff for any innovator.

The next step is to pinpoint the target customer and the target buyer. Often, these are not the same.

As in our prior chapter, we will first learn through simple frameworks and examples. Then, at the end of the chapter, we will ask you to apply these ideas to your own innovations ideas.

Learning Objectives

After reading this chapter you should be able to:

- Segment target customers by thinking about different groups for products and services in that market segment.

- For these customers, identify the most important use cases for products or services like yours.

- Determine which customer segment—that combination of customer group and product or service use case—which you wish to focus on first for your venture.

- Determine the size of the addressable market for your venture, e.g. the money presently being spent by your target customers on current solutions in your category, as well as how that market will grow in the next five years.

Creating a Customer Segmentation That Shows Users and Uses for the Types of Products or Services You Wish to Provide

The products and services of an innovation really matter. We design and build these products and services to please customers, and work just as hard figuring out the best to reach and sell these customers. Now, not all customers in the same in what they wish to buy in a certain category of products or services, or how they prefer to make their purchases. Understanding these differences – some of which are quite subtle – is very important for successful venturing.

Customer segmentation is the process of dividing a very broad group of potential customers into more specific groups, each with their own needs, attitudes, and preferences. It is the next step after performing a broader industry analysis.

Any given industry has major market segments. Different groups of customers exist within these segments, each of which might have multiple use cases for product or services like yours. Tennis, for example, has equipment manufacturers as one segment, and tennis clubs , tournaments, etc. as a services segment. Different types of customers include nonprofessional and professional players, who might be male or female, as well as the associations or clubs themselves. And, learning, recreational play, and tournament play might be the major use cases. As an innovator, you would think about specific products (such as a newer, better tennis ball) or services (such as analytics driven learning aids) that would target specific customers for specific use cases.

Figure 3.1 shows the customer segmentation grids for a B2C innovation within the snack foods industry sector. This customer segmentation was actually the basis for a wonderful corporate innovation that is a case study on our textbook Website, called MyMM'S. Go check it out! Or take a look at www.mymms.com. If you buy some, enjoy! There was a lot of careful thinking behind this innovation

Figure 3.1
A Customer
Segmentation
Grid for a
Chocolate Venture

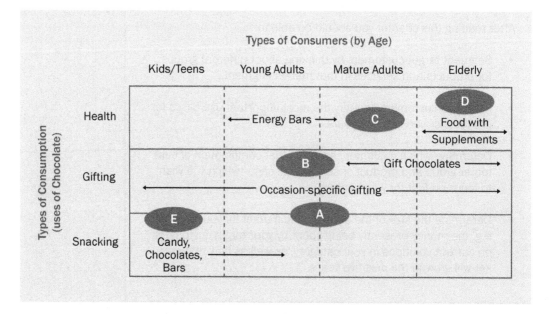

to transform a commodity candy product into a premium-priced service based on printing personalized candy. This is a fine example of **business model innovation.**

The axes for these customer segmentation grids need to be straightforward and meaningful. In the case of the snack food example in Figure 3.1, the horizontal axis shows different types of customers as measured by specific age groups. The reasoning behind using age as the basis for one of the axes is simply that people of different ages have different needs and preferences for snacking, be it for chocolate candies or anything else! The vertical axis in Figure 3.1 shows three major types of snack food consumption: snacking (or what we call "pigging out!" and which is an everyday sort of use for many consumers), gifting (as in giving chocolates to others for special occasions), and healthy snacking (which includes the energy bar segment). And each major use already has lots of current products in the marketplace, yet still offers considerable "white space" for innovation. The corporate innovation team used its own experience and judgment to define these three major uses and showed them to trusted colleagues for feedback and validation.

You can then overlay directly on top of a customer segmentation grid current products and circle what you perceive to be open market spaces. You can even put in current segment size and growth rates at the bottom or side of the grid. For example, for Figure 3.1, you could readily gather data on the current size and growth rate of the snack food segment, the gifting segment, and the healthy snacking segment, as well as the size and growth rates of the decennial age groups on the horizontal axis. The simple, single framework shown in Figure 3.1 then becomes a portal for all sorts of market, competitor, and opportunity pinpointing information. Any time you can present your team members or investors a simple, powerful picture rather than an entire memo or report, you are a winner!

Continuing with Figure 3.1, the competitive intensity facing an innovation trying to start a new candy company aimed at kids and teens for regular snacking is intense. You would be fighting world-class brands such as M&M'S Candies® Hershey's, or Snickers. Similarly, trying to start a gift chocolate company that competes directly with Godiva for the attention of mature adults would be difficult, simply because of that company's formidable branding and distribution presence. And taking PowerBar head on in the mainstream energy bar market for young adults is going to be tough—no matter how good your chefs and their recipes.

Innovators head for the "white space"—the adjacent areas in customer groups and basic product or service uses where there isn't much competition—or at least where the competition that exists is highly fragmented, e.g., a bunch of other small companies that are also trying to figure things out and scale up their respective businesses.

The innovator looks for open running room in a market. Continuing with Figure 3.1, you can see lots of running room. For example, innovators are now seeking to provide healthy drinks and snacks in the form of fortified water, bars, cookies, and dried vegetables for different types of consumers in the top row of our grid. In the second row of Figure 3.1, innovation in gifting is also pretty hot, with food and apparel companies like Vermont Teddy Bear bringing occasion-specific gifting ideas to market. And in the very first row of Figure 3.1, the traditional "pigging out" or snacking occasion, many food scientists working in companies large and small are trying to determine how to make more healthful yet still tasty snacks and treats. The obesity crisis is demanding change.

Importantly, remember that an innovator cannot focus on all three use occasions for consuming food as a single startup. It is just too hard in terms of product development and marketing. Above all else, the innovator needs to focus.

Focus applies to selecting an initial target customer group and the occasion of use or use case that will be the purpose of the innovation. To continue our food example, you can't make great tasty/healthy snacks for everyone—at least, not to start. Why not? Well, kids want different flavors and portion sizes than teens, and teens are different than the students reading this book; and you are very different than your parents. And the food itself is just one component. Marketing – the positioning and branding of the food product are very different for each target. Just consider the pictures and imagery shown for chocolates intended primarily for kids and teens, versus those for adults. And the distribution points are also often very different for different customer and use case combinations. Gift chocolates sell in one type of venue, energy bars in another, and regular candy in yet another.

In other words, getting specific about the customer group and the primary use for your intended products and services is fundamental for any innovation—both for your innovation planning and the execution of the plan once you start the company.

To complete our learning example from Figure 3.1, there are four distinct opportunities that the would-be food innovator might target to start an innovation:

- **Circle A:** Print customized, personalized printed candies for consumers of varying ages who are making purchases for different occasions. This was precisely the vision for the MyMM'S team, which looked at little kids' birthday parties, bar mitzvahs, graduations, weddings, ongoing romance (Valentine's Day), sporting events, and business uses such as recruiting, corporate training, and retirements. The basis for this business is to print text messages and jpegs on little, round M&M'S Candies®—ordered directly on the Web and shipped directly to the customers' house or place of business. And the venture charges at least ten times as much for these special candies as regular M&M'S Candies® sold at retail at checkout counters around the world

- **Circle B:** Develop a venture around a more contemporary type of gifting chocolate that would be "cool" for young adults still in college or just out of it (e.g., a much more contemporary type of Godiva). This is reflected by the positioning of Circle B on the grid at a younger crowd than Godiva. If you want to see an example of an entrepreneur who selected this as his target, visit www.mrchocolate.com, located, as you might suspect, in Manhattan, New York. Women consumers, particularly young professional women (or those who remain young at heart) absolutely relish his creations!

- **Circle C:** Develop a venture around health or energy bar products that have great taste, are less fattening for mature adults, and have functional supplements. For example, most energy bars have high caloric density—and don't taste all that great. A new, great-tasting energy bar product might be positioned for older, "aspirational" athletes, reflected by the positioning of Circle C.

- **Circle D:** A venture might also make functional bars for the region labeled Circle D, such as a great-tasting, portioned or tabbed chocolate bar loaded up with calcium and other ingredients designed to improve bone strength for mature women.

- **Circle E:** Or we might decide to fly right into the face of the established competition in the kids/teens snacking market, trying to add to or disrupt the established confectionary business. For example, we might try to make healthy snacks that are both really good for kids and that they love to eat! There is a need for "fun fruit"—a whole serving of fruits, without heavy sugars, in different kid-friendly flavors and kids-designed packaging. Moms still have trouble getting their kids to eat fresh fruit, so this concept might be an answer for the lunch box.

In this example, there are plenty of opportunities that emerge from the process of customer segmentation. And we could do the same thing for drinks – around which there has been so much innovation in this category in recent years. The lesson here is that you can be an innovator even in what appears to be a mature, stable category if you do your segmentation carefully, work hard to understand customers' frustrations with current solutions, and design creatively to meet those needs.

The above example has been for a consumer-oriented business (B2C). For a business-to-business innovation (B2B), innovators typically start segmenting customers by (a) industries or vertical markets, and (b) size of company. A software company might segment its customers into financial services, retail, healthcare, and manufacturing companies, and then by size of company—small, medium, and large—within these vertical markets. The innovator might then further focus by saying that he or she wishes to concentrate on providing CRM (customer relationship management) and analytics to small businesses doing eCommerce on the Web, and provide these analytics through the Cloud as a service. (If you do that, make sure that you have competitive differentiation from a really hot Boston company called HubSpot!)

Once you have a customer – use case focus, you can then concentrate on the rest of the innovation: the design of solutions for customers, the route to market, how to communicate value or otherwise brand products and services, how to charge for these solutions and make operate that particular business profitably. Customer segmentation and carefully targeting translates directly into improving the Customer Value Proposition you created in Chapter 1.

A Customer Segmentation Example for Services

Some of you in the course will be thinking about innovations that are services-related, as opposed to product-based. Customer segmentation works just as well for services as it does for products. Let's take the following example.

Suppose that you want to start a travel services business. We have a group of former students who are travel innovators. Members of this team had worked or done

Customer Segmentation Should Be Meaningful, Measureable, and Actionable

As this travel service and the prior chocolate examples show, it is also important to keep customer segmentation within your industry section simple, easy to explain to others, and still powerful in terms of providing clear vision into the different possible types of customers and their uses for your types of products or services. This will make your strategy easier to explain to partners, employees, and investors. It will also be easier to explain to your professor!

For these reasons, we try to limit customer segmentation grids to just two, and at most three, dimensions. It is fairly easy to explain phenomena that have two major dimensions. Once we get into three, it becomes a lot harder!

How do you know that your customer segmentation grid is a good one for planning a new venture? Here are some pointers:

The axes and the boundary points in the axes must be meaningful to you and your team members. By meaningful, we mean that the axes are not obtuse or vague. For example, differences in consumer ages have impact in whatever you are proposing to do; differences in industry category have impact; differences in geography have impact. A customer segmentation grid must be able to speak for itself to the viewer.

Your axes must be measurable and researchable: for example, age groups and genders. Industries, size of companies, and geographies are measurable in the sense that you can find data on the current size and growth rates of these segments. And the use case axis on your grid must be either current known uses for products or services in your type of business, or ones that industry observers regard as highly likely to exist in the future. Home medical monitoring, smart home energy management, and rooftop organic greenhouse vegetable growing are all examples of fundamental use cases whose time will come!

Your customer segmentation grid must be actionable. This means it must show open running room, a clear path for innovation and venturing, such as we saw in Figure 2.1. If it is not actionable, then try a different design. Define your customer groups and uses in a more creative way where white space comes forth. The first design of a customer segmentation grid is rarely the last. This takes careful thought and usually a few iterations.

internships for major travel agencies, had lived abroad for a bit, and were very enthusiastic about starting their own business. They had a clear need to focus on a segment within the enormous travel business. Going to www.ustravel.org, they quickly saw two major customer segments and major use cases: leisure travelers and business travelers, traveling either domestically or abroad.

For leisure travel in the United States alone, they found that the segment size was valued at over $560 billion in 2011; that three-quarters of domestic trips were for leisure purposes; and that U.S. residents logged over 1.5 billion person-trips for leisure travel during that year, with primary "uses" being to visit relatives, to shop, to visit friends, and to do rural sightseeing and visit beaches. For business travel, the numbers were almost $250 billion in travel by U.S. residents during 2011, and 458 million person-trips. Then there is the "international" travel use occasion: In 2011, travel spending by Americans abroad totaled over $110 billion, and foreign visitors spent close to $153 billion visiting the United States. Overall, there was 9% growth of travel to Asia and the Pacific, 8% growth to Africa as well as the Middle East, 6% growth to Europe, and 4% growth for travel to the United States. For such a large existing industry, these were indeed impressive numbers. For your own term projects, think about where you might find this type of granular industry data. It reads well in a business plan!

With these data, the team looked to its own personal knowledge and experience, and decided to go after U.S. residents traveling abroad—at least a $110 billion a year market. For specific customer groups, the team then used an age/lifestyle approach for its segmentation: college students traveling (and studying) abroad, young professionals without children, young families, Baby Boomers, and seniors. They noted further that, while there are major players handling enormous chunks of business (through Web portals, the airlines, or the hotel companies), there was only fragmented competition focused on the international travel business. As they considered international travel further, they found some significant competitors serving mature adults and families, (such as Thomson Safaris, featured in Outside magazine's 2012 Active Travel Award & All-Time Favorite Trips Hall of Fame.) But there didn't seem to be major players directly targeting younger U.S. travelers, Millenials, where international travel would seem to be a more natural fit. Understanding the semester study abroad concept, the team focused first on college students and began its field research with students on their old college campuses and elsewhere.

The team created a new line of services in international travel—safe yet fun, and also educational—for college students studying abroad. Industry reports also showed this to be a booming part (we can call it a niche) within the leisure travel industry segment. The Travel Industry Association of America has estimated that about 10% of Americans have taken an international travel trip, and that this is growing by about 10% a year. 10% of the broader segment of $110 billion is $11 billion – and that became the innovation team's addressable market. If they were even able to capture in the range of 5% of that market, revenues would approach $50 million a year. Several members of the team moved to Italy to arrange some weekends and week-long trips to interesting venues in Africa and Eastern Europe, while others stayed in the United States to market directly to students and university administrators. Soon the team was selling to dozens of universities and providing hundreds of trips to Americans studying abroad in major European cities. If you would like to read more, go to our textbook Website and grab the SnoworSand case.

Established Market Segments Versus Emerging Industry Niches

When we hear that an innovator has "created an industry," what they have really done is to create a tiny new niche in an established market segment that is part of a much bigger industry. That tiny niche then grows over time becomes quite large. Fred Smith of Federal Express started with a couple of airplanes delivering mail overnight. Now expedited delivery is a global industry.

People who have the vision and courage to create new niches within an industry are nothing short of business geniuses. Take Steve Jobs. Jobs created three new industries, each with multiple market segments, comprised of smaller niches. First, there was desktop publishing with the Mac and PageMaker software. Second, Jobs created computer-generated animation for movies by starting Pixar. And third, most people think he initiated media convergence, by conceiving and bringing to market services such as iTunes and mobile hardware such as the iPod and iPhone. Pure genius, three times over.

The great thing about emerging niche with a segment of an established industry is that competition tends to be highly fragmented. The market is there for the taking. The bad thing is that customers are not yet spending lots of money for products or services in that niche—because there are few if any yet to be had! The innovator has to be both an excellent innovator and businessperson to drive and service customer demand.

With some luck, good product, and great marketing, the innovator might find his or her little niche "taking off" to become major market segments in its own right. Consider the example of eBay, now a multibillion-dollar business with operations in over 30 countries. It was founded by Pierre Omidvar, who had started a business called AuctionWeb in 1995. Omidvar discovered that there were collectors of all sorts of odd items scanning the world for things to purchase. He perceived the Web as a great way to connect buyers with sellers without having to go to antique stores, fairs, and the like. Now online auctioning is an important segment for consumer purchasing. It has also become widely used in certain types of industrial buying, known as Internet auctions. Corporations will put procurements for either products or services into an online auction, often forcing suppliers to bid down to the winning price.

If the innovator is an entrepreneur, and can successfully launch a product or service into an emerging niche, then grow the business, he or she might have the opportunity to dominate that niche as it becomes larger and larger. At that point, the entrepreneur has options: the innovation will probably become an acquisition target by a corporation that is a lead player in the larger market "segment"; or the innovation might have the revenues and profitability needed to do an initial public offering, raising the cash needed to either do its own R&D or make acquisitions to grow into adjacent market segments. This idea of finding an emerging niche, innovating successfully, and marketing better than competitors is a tried and true path to successful innovation and entrepreneurship.

In contrast to pioneering emerging market niches, many innovators decide to work in existing market segments with new products and services. The pathway to success here is that the innovator must beat current competitors with truly better products or services, better marketing, and/or a new business model that hits the customer's sweet spot. Clearly, the nice thing about innovating in an established market segment is that there is already customer money flowing into the purchase of the products and services. The bad thing for the innovator is that there is established competition, often lots of it! To win, you have to be extra-differentiated in the design of your products and services, in your marketing, and in how you do business with customers. And you might have to be price aggressive in order to convince existing resellers and end-customers to swap out other products for yours. That means smaller operating margins and the need to get more customers faster in order to have a successful business compared to new products and services for which there is less competition, and therefore less price sensitivity.

The Importance of Finding Innovative Customers

It is important to find customers who have innovative attitudes and behaviors, who desire new solutions, and who appreciate the benefits of those solutions for improving their lives and businesses. To create a "hot" innovative company, find those customers who want to taste your hot sauce. These are customers who want to try the new—or at least to test the new.

For consumer products, this means finding retail customers who enjoy trying new products like yours in a store or online. Or, for services ventures, try to find those smart customers who want "smarter" services. For example, in the commercial building energy segment, the entrepreneur would try to find building owners who are convinced that the sensors and software for "smarter builds" can help save energy expenses and reduce maintenance costs. Or, if you are into healthcare, it could be the Chief Medical Officers of large hospitals who are just dying (sorry for the pun!) to use interactive Web conference technology to keep patients on proper rehabilitation after leaving the hospital. This prevents hospital readmissions (which are expensive), and as well as being good for patients. Indeed, while there are many exciting places to start a company— you need to find and partner with actual customers who are excited by new possibilities as you, and who are willing to give their time to help design and test solutions. These customers are sometimes called "lead users."[1]

Some market segments are ripe with innovative customers. That's a great thing for the entrepreneur. Innovative customers actually like to try and even pay for brand-new products or services as part of their overall professional and personal makeup[2]. They are innovators, themselves. For the entrepreneur, such customers will help you fine-tune your initial product or service to make it even better for the broader market. Second, any entrepreneur will tell you that the sales cycle for bringing new revenue in the door is one of the most painful realities facing a new company. Shorten your sales cycle—particularly for a technology-intensive product—and you are well on your way to a successful business. Innovative customers tend buy quicker, if they have the cash. Third, these customers seek to build partnerships with entrepreneurs, one based on trust and respect that goes both ways. They will not beat you down on price. They will also look to you for your next set of solutions. And perhaps most important, they will serve as references to future customers. You can put their names on your Website, for example. You can even have a few new customers call them as part of a sale. They will also voluntarily spread the word about your company. All of this is pure gold for the entrepreneur. But again, you must deliver. An early customer's respect must be earned.

---

1 Von Hippel, E. (1988). The Sources of Innovation. Oxford, England: Oxford University Press.

2 Moore, G. A. (1999). Crossing the Chasm: Marketing and Selling High-Tech Products to Mainstream Customers. New York: Harper Business Essentials.

So discover the lead users within your target market segment. Who are they? What do they need? How much will they spend? What other products or services might they want to use with yours? Think "partnership."[3] Find them and go talk to them. Don't be shy!

Defining Your Own Customer Groups

Now let's start building the customer segmentation grid for your innovation. It is the next step after defining your target industry and gathering higher level industry and competitive data in the prior chapter. One axis is going to be major types or groups of customers; the other, major types of uses or use cases for your intended products or services. It is this intersection of major customer groups and major use cases that we will think of as a market segment. As but another example, drug discovery innovations tend to segment their markets by type of disease (the user), and the use cases of diagnostics, cure, and prevention. Then, they will focus on one type of disease -- and within that, one variant of that disease – and then get into diagnostic kits or actual therapies, e.g. earlier stage detection of cancer, or some new type of cancer treatment.

Once you have these customer groups and use cases defined, you can then begin digging deeper into the needs and preferences of a specific set of customers needed to create the products, services, and business model for your innovation.

Look at Figure 3.2. We want you to begin to complete this figure for your own innovation.

You do not need to find a large number of different types of customers in a given target industry. In most cases, you will find two or three distinct groups. And, if the buyers are not the end-users, you should create a second version of Figure 3.2 that focuses just on the different types of buyers within your market segment. For a food product innovation, for example, the customers could be you or I, but the actual buyer segments being mass merchandizers (Walmart, Target), grocery chains (Krogers, Publix, Safeway), and specialty retailers (Wholefoods, Trader Joe's, Sprouts). It is important to understand the differences between buyers as well as users.

---

3 Von Hippel, E. (1988). The Sources of Innovation, Oxford, England: Oxford University Press; Von Hippel, E. (2005). "The best way to innovate? Let lead users do it for you" Inc Magazine, September.

Figure 3.2
Identifying Different Types of Customers in an Industry

Customer Group	Description of Typical Customer Needs and Behaviors (Use bullet points)	Segment Size/Share (Use words or actual numbers)	Priority in Terms of Startup Focus

Figure 3.3 provides some helpful hints for completing Figure 3.2. We have included key words or data elements that you might find useful: one set for "B2C" innovations, where you are selling things to consumers; and another set for "B2B" innovations, where you are selling things to businesses or government organizations. Simply create a name for the specific customer group and then start to gather information for the various bullet points under the column that best represents your type of business. That will include the following:

• Indicate the specific end-user and buyer for your products or services

• Gather demographic or industry information

• Determine the decision-making level of the buyers: Who are they? What power or influence do they have in the purchase decision?

• Lastly, identify the primary needs and behaviors of end-users within the customer group

Once we have a handle on the major types of customers by virtue of their core needs and behaviors, we can then say with greater confidence which customer group we wish to serve, and for which use case we are specifically targeting.

There needs to be a good reason for your target customer, use-case selection. For example, let's say that you have chosen a specific customer group because it values high-quality products and services, appreciates good design, and is less likely to purchase just on price. You have found a number of lead users in that customer group willing to experiment with your new products or services. Or, you might have found that a certain use case within a customer group is the fastest growing in the industry. For example, mobile apps for health, fitness, and nutrition are super

	Business to Consumer	Business to Business
Consumer Group Name		
User Type	• Buying for self • Buying for others • Using what others have bought for me	• Buying for self • Buying for others • Using what others have bought for me
Demographics	• Age, income, gender, marital status • Health condition (for some categories) • Geography/ Culture (for some categories)	• Industry–vertical market/segment • Size of organization • Status–profit/nonprofit
Decision-Making Level	• Head of household • Influencer • None of the above	• Business unit/department • Rank and authority • Role in buying decision
Needs & Behaviors	• Physical activities around product/ service use • Used alone or with others • Attitudes and emotions, positive and negative • Only buys at certain occasions during the year	• Focused on revenue growth • Focused on reducing operating expenses • Risk-taking versus conservative • Only buys at certain times in the budget cycle

Figure 3.3
Factors to Consider When Describing Target Customers

hot right now. You might have found that there is a particular customer group that is stuck with a specific problem and is literally crying out for help. New technologies for homeland security to counter new threats might be an example of this. You need to frame your segment selection based on your industry and customer research. Investors will need to hear *that story*.

Application of Customer Segmentation to New Services: Farming of the Future

These frameworks apply equally well to corporate innovations. We hope that some of you in the class are considering or already working for a major corporation where the executives are supportive of new internal venturing and innovation. This example is for you.

Let's populate the Customer Segmentation Template from one such case. A few years ago, we came across a corporate innovation team seeking to create software services for agricultural farming management. This multi-billion dollar company had forever been in the "product business," but this internal innovation team wanted to move into "services."

Figure 3.4
Farmer Customer Segmentation—The Major Groups in Grains Production, data circa 2010

Customer Group Label	Description/Persona	Segment Size/Share	Priority/Status
Steady Eddie	Wants to stay the same if possible, stay profitable, sell the farm in 5-10 years and move to someplace warm in the winter. Thinks intuitively. If he doesn't use a computer to run the business now, he is never likely to.	About 35% of US acres for grain growing, and 160,000 farms Declining share	May be large in market share, but not a good target
Up & Comer	Thinker, Planner, Tester. A Performance Maximizer. Trained to use computers to manage business. Likely attended an agriculture college and may have an MBA. Trades commodities. Tracks inputs/outputs acre by acre.	20% of US acres, about 70,000 farms Growing share fast	#1 Top Target User
Sun Downer	Part-time farmers. Running the farm as a life style choice, not to make money. May use computers in the city, but the farm is an escape from technology. Price focused in buying seed and equipment.	About 10% US acres, About 35,000 farms Growing slowly	Not a target
Livestock Farmer	Looks for quality, but growing grains is not the top priority. Might be interested in a service to take the problem off his hands, but using his land. Includes dairy, poultry, and pork farmers.	14% of US acres, 89,000 35% Stable	#2 Priority Find 3rd parties who grow grains on their land.

The industry was the production of hybrid seeds for growing agricultural crops to be fed to livestock. The team's vision was to expand the business from just growing seeds to providing a comprehensive set of agronomic and analytical services to help farmers get the most out of their land, including using the correct type of seeds, fertilizers, and insecticides for each specific acre of land in the farm. This is farming of the future – and it is already happening. Innovators are developing computerized services that would match soil quality with agricultural inputs with harvested outputs.

The team thought it best to focus on the larger farms—those with more than 10,000 acres of land under management. The initial product idea was to create a software tool that would allow the farm owner to specify all grain farm inputs (seed types and quality, pesticides, herbicides, planting and harvesting machines, etc.) and agricultural outputs, and monitor profit and productivity to better plan the next growing season. This tool would be provided as a "hosted" service to farmers because the customer wasn't expected to have fancy computer systems.

Over the coming months, team members visited a dozen farming operations in their state. Those visits revealed four distinct types of grain farmers, shown in Figure 3.4. There were farmers who followed traditional methods, called "Steady Eddies." Then there were "Performance Optimizers," younger farmers who were comfortable with computers and who truly ran their farms as growing businesses. The team also visited weekend farmers, the Sun Downers, as well as the Dairy Farmers whose only interest was to grow corn to feed their livestock. The team took photographs of these customers and developed "personas" for each farmer type. A persona is a fancy way of referring to a set of bullet points that describes the attitudes, behaviors, needs, and preferences for a particular type of customer. The team then went to the Web and found federal government sources that provided data on size, growth rates, and trends in each customer group. All this is shown in Figure 3.4. The team then decided to target the innovative farmer—the Performance Maximizer—with its new suite of analytic services.

Take a good look at the figure because this is what we believe you need to create for your innovation! In this case, the Performance Maximizer was the rapidly customer group with plenty of innovative customers. You will probably want the same thing for your innovation.

Digging More into Interesting Use Cases for Target Customers

Now, lets look at specific use cases more carefully.

Consider Urban Outfitters. The very successful U.S. retailer has different brands to suit different customers and use cases. Urban Outfitters targets young, educated, urban-minded women and men in the 18- to 30-year-old range buying clothes; Anthropologie brings a global, cultural artfulness to older professional female consumers looking for clothes and home furnishings; and Terrain provides outdoor furnishings for affluent, mature females. Urban Outfitters also created BHLDN, a retail concept that focuses on contemporary wedding dresses and accessories for

Figure 3.5
Customer
Segmentation:
Types of Customers
and Types of Use
Cases

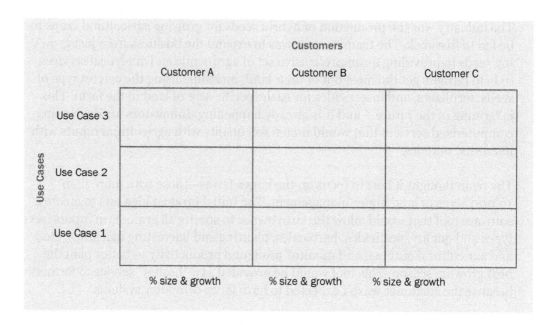

women. Each one of these retail brands serves a different customer and use case combination. They represent innovations targeting different market segments.

Or, for a business-to-business example, look to IBM. It divides its marketplace into more than a dozen major industries, each with specific segments. For example, IBM segments the financial services industry into retail and commercial banking, insurance, and investment banking. Then, across these segments, it creating solutions for taking out operating costs, running assets more efficiently, or growing revenue. IBM tunes its solutions for these use cases to its different industry verticals. For example, IBM has specific analytic solutions for the marketing departments of banks and telecommunications companies trying to win new customers and up-sell current ones. Or, its smarter city solutions are targeting crime and safety, traffic management, and citizen services as specific use cases for public sector customers. It is all about focusing on specific customers and use cases. This is a very powerful, focusing framework for both large companies and startups.

This customers and use case framework yields the picture shown in Figure 3.5. On the horizontal axis are distinct groups of customers as we have defined them above. Any information that you can gather—from the government databases, magazine articles, or trade associations—on the size and growth rate of these major customer groups is important because it can help you better focus on a particular customer group.

The vertical axis of Figure 3.5 is use cases. Different use cases for a food company might be breakfast, lunch, dinner, and snacking; and then, "at home" or "on the go" (for customers of different ages and genders). For a software security company, use cases include data center security, desktop security, and mobile security (for individuals, SME, and large corporate or government customers). For a healthcare innovation, primary use cases include hospital-based care, ambulatory care (e.g., walk-in clinics), and home care for customers varying by age and severity of disease (and, in the United States, type of insurance). Again, as the innovator, this customers-use case segmentation framework allows you to pinpoint your innovations.

Identifying Different Customers and Use Cases for Enterprise Software

We once worked with a venture-capital-backed software team that was nonetheless stuck in its tracks. Its customer segmentation included financial services firms, Telco's, and data service bureaus, all of whom used the company's device-independent "storage management" software. This software reconnoitered across the large computer networks of major corporations (using EMC, IBM, HP, Sun, and Hitachi for storage devices) to find where data were stored, how much data were stored, and how frequently the data were accessed. The software produced massive reports that created a graphic map of where big companies were storing all the various data around the world. Pretty impressive. But the software was only used by database administrators in IT departments, and they didn't have a lot of money to spend on anything.

We took a few of the lead engineers out into the field to visit key enterprise customers. As we poked around, we observed a fundamental use case that
no one was solving at the time. This was to produce data that could be used to "charge-back" departments within a large company for their use of centralized computer storage and services. The CIO of a large enterprise could find out which departments were using centralized services and then meter that use and charge the user-departments for their activity. This was the beginning of the shared services computing model—what today we call Cloud computing. We realized that chargeback could put money back into the pockets of the CIOs.

The venture set about the work of creating the first chargeback software for enterprise storage. A year later, this same venture—called Highground Systems—was purchased for more than 8X sales—over $400 million! That chargeback use-case for the CIO customer was killer!

For enterprise software entrepreneurs reading this book, we encourage you to work "up" the customers' organization, find users with clout and money, and innovate for them.

Rarely can the innovator identify all the current and new, emerging use cases among a set of customers by just sitting behind his or her desk. You need to get out and enter the world of the customer. You already have your major customer groups from the work above. You need to determine where these representative customers exist and how best to visit them. Web browsing doesn't work here; your research needs to be face to face. Go where these different types of customers actually use products or services like yours, and then, also visit where customers buy those products. You will learn so much.

Go to these places for an hour or two to watch, listen, and learn. Important use cases will come to light—we guarantee it. And from these, you will truly begin to innovate. That's another guarantee.

One of your author's very first companies was a software innovation that made real-time software for manufacturing process control for brewing beer. We actually became the market leader in this category. But to achieve success we had to visit large breweries, live and in-person, to learn the industrial environment, the variety of temperature and pressure sensors we needed to integrate, the types of specific information and automation plant operators needed for their jobs, and the daily and weekly information needed by plant managers on production runs. Only then, armed with these very specific use cases modeled with the "brewery process control" target, could we build the correct and necessary software. Another benefit, of course, was that we were also able to sample our customers' products, e.g., their beer!

Sizing the Addressable Market for a Venture

Individuals and organizations that invest in innovations typically want to know the size of your addressable market. The addressable market is simply the current amount of money flowing from the purchase of current products and services by your target customers your target use cases. Then, investors will want to know how fast the segment is growing. In short, the addressable market is a revenue projection based on industry and customer purchasing data.

Innovation capital firms would like to see a business plan that shows an addressable market of $1 billion over the coming five years, because if the innovation takes 10% of that revenue, it will be a $100 million plus revenue business. Angel investors will typically be attracted to less grandiose visions, say a $200-300 million addressable market. Either way, in most technology sectors, innovations can be sold for 4 to 5 times revenue, which tends to lead to very healthy return on investment for the outside investors.

If you would like to see a clear example of defining an addressable market, take a look at the SilverRail Technologies case on this book's Website. The entrepreneur started a business to aggregate open high-speed train travel seats across different countries in Europe, and present these as a single booking and financial transaction to consumers, typically through travel portals. He started with a $300 billion worldwide train travel market, of which $80 billion was in Europe. He then focused only on rail travel lasting between two and four hours, his "sweet spot" in terms of replacing discount plane travel in Europe. That opportunity gap represented an addressable market of initially $22 billion. Only 13% of that $22 billion ticket revenue was being booked online due to a lack of a seat aggregator. The entrepreneur's goal was to get that number to 60% comparable to that of on-line train booking in the United States. If he could capture that extra 47%, with a 5% booking commission, the company would grow to about $150 million in revenue. It was a compelling opportunity. To date, he has raised more than $40 million for the innovation and is beginning to achieve scale through Europe.

As stated by the entrepreneur:

When pitching investors, it's very important not to talk about tackling the whole market, but to segment the market down into something more believable and achievable—it builds credibility with the VCs who are tired of companies pitching them on how they're going to "capture just 2% of the total market," which is simply not a believable approach. If you talk about tackling the whole market, you're going to get kicked out of the room. The more detailed you are in your segmentation, the more credibility you gain.

Get real data wherever you can, and then, make the numbers work for you. Make the numbers help tell the story about the attractiveness of your business.

In this chapter, we have shown you how to identify different types of customers within a target industry segment, and to then find specific use cases for these customers. It is the combination of customer and use case that makes for a target market segment. This then becomes the basis for determining your addressable market. And, for the next chapter, customer segmentation and targeting becomes the basis for face-to-face, intimate customer research. In the next chapter, we will learn how understand how customers think, feel, and act within specific use cases.

READER EXERCISES

Step 1: Spend Some Time With Your Target Customers and Their Uses

Create the Customers and Their Uses Template for your own innovation. Remember, you have already selected an industry focus and the type of business you want to create from the prior chapter. Now we begin to dig deeper into that target industry segment/niche to develop a further focus on the types of problems you want to solve, and for whom you wish to solve them.

a. Label the columns and rows for the Customers and Their Use Cases (Figure 3.6) for your venture. That means identifying the specific customer groups and their primary uses for products or services, such as the ones you might create.

b. Take a quick visit (if possible) to your different customer groups in their places of work or leisure. Spend an hour with each. Observe. See the primary use cases. Look for emerging use cases (such as virtual training versus face-to-face training for complex computer systems).

c. After constructing your customer segmentation grid, circle your primary customer and use combination. Start crafting the story behind why your customer target makes so much sense.

Figure 3.6
Customer
Segmentation:
Set Your Initial
Target Customer
and Use Case/
Occasion

Customers

	Customer A	Customer B	Customer C
Use Case 3			
Use Case 2			
Use Case 1			
	% size & growth	% size & growth	% size & growth

Use Cases

- *Label the rows and columns*
- *Put in the relative size and growth rate for each Customer Group*
- *Put in the relative value or spending of each Customer Group*
- *Circle your target Customer and Use*

Step 2: Size Your Addressable Market

Next, hit the Web and try to find data for the relative size and spending for your target customer group and use case. Take another look at the travel industry fact sheet in the Tip Box provided in the prior chapter. Maybe you will be fortunate enough to find lots of data in a single, convenient source. Otherwise, keep digging and assemble the data yourself. Investors are definitely going to want to know the following:

1. The size of your target market segment within your industry, e.g. your specific customer group in the use cases upon which you plan to focus.

2. How you see your see that market size growing over the coming five years

Think about the rail travel booking service example earlier in this chapter. The entrepreneur started with a very broad market (European train travel), got more specific (high-speed rail between two and four hours), and then got even more specific (another 50% or so that might be booked online) to size his "addressable market." He then estimated reasonable penetration rates and applied a standard 5% booking commission to get some revenue projections. He did a "top-down" revenue projection. That's what we want you to get started on now. You cannot have a good business plan without a strong rationale for your revenue projections.

Later, in the Reality Check described towards the end of this book, we will teach you another method for revenue projection that is based on actually surveying prospective customers in your market segment. You will find their level of dissatisfaction with existing solutions, their "purchase intent" for your new solution, and how much they are willing to spend on your solution. We call this a "bottoms-up" approach to revenue projection. In reality, the innovator needs to try to do both the top-down and bottoms-up approaches to market sizing and revenue projection, and then compare the results.

But for now, get started with the top-down approach. You need a healthy market to support all your hard work. This exercise is going to help you see if that is the case. If it doesn't feel sufficiently large, use your customer segmentation grid to explore adjacent segments/niches, or alternative or additional uses to enlarge the pie.

	Improvement, or Substantial Pivot
ABC (give it a name) is our product / solution	
That (solves what problem)	
For (which target customers)	
For (which target buyers)	
The benefits we expect to provide (name the major benefits) will make ABC stand out from similar products and/or services.	
And is different than current (competitors/products) because of (why customers will buy it)	
Now, put it all together:	

Figure 3.7
Improving the Customer Value Proposition

Step 3: Refine Your Customer Value Proposition

Take a look at the Customer Value Proposition for your innovation from the prior chapter. Improve it with your thinking and field research about customers and use cases. What have you learned from your initial customer visits? If you have not done any customer visits yet, start doing them! The customer is the source of truth. From this, do you have a better idea about the products or services your might provide, the benefits for customers, and the differentiation against competitors? Sharpen your pencil. Improve your Customer Value Proposition!

If you have learned that your idea is not a particularly good one, do what most innovators do early and often: PIVOT. Figure 3.7 can help you think about pivoting towards a more refined and better Customer Value Proposition. Fill it out and show it to your professors, friends, and partners. Pivoting shows that you are learning.

DEVELOPING THE PRODUCT OR SERVICE CONCEPT:
User centered design to improve the total experience

4

The Purpose of the Chapter

The previous chapter helped you segment your customers into different groups and their basic types of uses for your category of products or services, e.g. their use cases. We then had you select your initial focus—the combination of customer group and use case—as the basis for understanding customer needs. Now we move on to the business of how to quickly and effectively understand those needs. We call this getting into the hearts and minds of target users and target buyers. The two—users and buyers—are not always the same, but both are essential for getting a handle on "the customer" for any innovation team.

As in prior chapters, we will include a few basic frameworks and help illustrate them with examples. Then, in the Reader Exercises, we will ask you to apply these frameworks to your own innovation—in this case, to do in-depth customer research.

Learning Objectives

- Refine your understanding of customer needs, with a clear distinction between users and buyers

- Develop the first design of your product or service based on those needs

- Take a first crack at defining the "value" customers will find in your solutions, be it functional, economic, emotional, or social

User Centered, Improve the Experience-based Design

In general, the innovator—either as entrepreneur or corporate innovator—wants to create powerful products or services that dramatically improve the customer's experience. Any experience is part of a specific use case. For example, Starbucks innovated the customer's experience of going to a coffee shop by adding a comfortable, den-like environment and wireless connectivity to excellent coffee products. MyMM'S—the customer-printed candy case found on our textbook Website—transformed the chocolate gifting experience by allowing consumers to print messages and pictures directly onto M&M'S Candies.® The specific use cases tend to be birthdays, graduations, weddings, romance, and retirements. Similarly, the GPS and social networking technology flooding into cars can dramatically improve the driver's experience for certain key use occasions—such as avoiding traffic jams or finding stores with certain types of products and promotions. Target the customer, get specific about certain use cases, learn the user's problems and frustrations, and then think of ways to improve the experience. The innovator needs to do this to create differentiated products and services.

Getting Ready to Jump Into the Hearts and Minds of Your Customers

Many companies get started because the innovator, in one way or another has been "the user" and "the buyer" for the type of product or service he or she wants to create. As a representative user in the field, the innovator recognizes the critical flaws in existing products and services, sees the gap in the marketplace for something better, and proceeds forward. Many of you reading this book may be such users already. You may be frustrated with what you have in your target industry segment/niche, and have already thought deeply about the design and performance of what you believe could be a much better solution.

For example, one of our closest friends and mentors, Al Lehnerd, was a senior manager at Black & Decker. Al had six kids. His wife left for a church retreat for an entire weekend, leaving Al alone with all of their kids for two days straight. After 48 hours of nonstop cleaning, including plugging in the vacuum cleaner a dozen times, Al went to work with a pain in his back on Monday morning. In just a few days, he designed and prototyped a portable vacuum cleaner that didn't have to be plugged in, the Dustbuster!

However, even if you are like Al and have a brilliant personal insight as a frustrated user of current products and services in your target industry area, remember that you still need to validate your idea with other customers. You need to talk with a number of them to make sure that your pain is also *their pain*. As a fellow user, it should be pretty easy for you to start a conversation, commiserate, and learn more.

If you personally are not representative of the target customer in market segment, no worries. We are going to learn how to observe, interview, and generally interact with target customers in a way that is highly productive for you and not threatening to them.

From the prior chapter, you have circled that combination of customer group and use case(s) that you will focus on for the work in this chapter. Now you simply need to find where these customers exist at work or leisure, observe them, and then, with certain methods, talk to them. We guarantee that you will uncover their fears, frustrations, and concerns. It is then up to you to create the product or service solutions that address these needs, and then the business model best suited for your solutions. Solving an important need or frustration in your customers makes your solutions a "must-buy" for them, as opposed to a "nice-to-buy"—and this is what you need for a successful innovation.

Also, in practice, many teams find themselves investigating several closely adjacent customer groups and use cases before deciding on the one best suited for their innovation team. They do the field research of this chapter on a couple of different targets, and let the research itself drive their final decision. It sounds like more work, but it can be well worth the effort if you are serious about starting a company. At this stage of the game, it is most important to experiment—to try a few different ideas and see which one is best. Be open to being told by a customer that your initial idea is simply wrong or misguided; and, in that process, invariably you might learn what might indeed be a better idea. Innovators learn from trial and error.

Doing the Field Research: Learning About the Attitudes, Behaviors, and Core Needs of Target Customers

Armed with some initial ideas for innovative solutions for customer needs, your key to success from this point forward is to identify and spend time with several or more target users and buyers. Insight cannot be gained remotely. Communication over the telephone or through e-mail removes the intimacy of observation and the nonverbal expression that lies at the heart of identifying and understanding a customer's pain and frustrations. You are going to have to roll up your sleeves and "exist" with them for short but concentrated periods of time to get your true "Aha!"

Understanding the customers' frustrations with current products or services in your chosen market niche is an essential element of a new business opportunity. Finding these frustrations, paying particular attention to knowledgeable, thoughtful customers, pays rich dividends.

If your fieldwork does not unearth any clear customer frustrations, do not despair. Continue to look at the edges around your initial focus. Pivot. Rarely are there no problems to solve.

Spending time with customers helps you think more deeply about the business you could create and the products and services it might offer. More often, it will provide you with a direct indication of desirable products, services, pricing, and strategies for beating current competitors. Moreover, investors will know in a second if you are smart about your target customers.

Do not expect this customer research to be something that you can put off until two days before your class meeting when presentations are due. It takes time to plan your attack, to conduct the meetings, and to synthesize the results. Reaching out to customers does not come naturally to some innovators, especially to those with strong technical backgrounds. Get over it. You and your team need to be deeply grounded in the world of your target customers—for products, services, and business model development.

Moreover, innovation does not exist in a vacuum. Customers will often tell you that they like the products and services that already exist in the marketplace from your competitors[1]. This is because the fierce, competitive nature of our economy has already driven most inferior products and services from the field. Truly bad choices have probably been purged from the marketplace. Therefore, your innovation will have to supplant current products and services that have some good points. Your new product, service, or even business model design must be distinctive in some clear way. For many innovation teams, this distinctive edge comes in the design and functionality of the products or services. For others, the edge comes in the go-to-market aspect of the business—such as the best sales force or the coolest Website. And yet for a few others, the competitive advantage comes in the approach to pricing. An example might be creating a powerful software application that saves customers demonstrable amounts of time and money. Instead of charging them a hefty licensing fee, the company requests a percentage of the time and money saved. Whatever the method, your solutions must be distinctive for customers and differentiated from current competitors.

Some technologists believe that they can think their way to breakthrough business concepts from the comfort of their labs or offices. They are uneasy with the prospect of meeting with strangers and listening to people who have much less technical knowledge than they do. However, technologists cannot assume that they know what is best for customers. Customers will guide technologists towards the best applications for any given technology. Innovation needs to be rooted in improving the experience of the target user.

Some technologists believe that they can think their way to breakthrough business concepts from the comfort of their labs or offices. They are uneasy with the prospect of meeting with strangers and listening to people who have much less technical knowledge than they do. However, technologists cannot assume that they know what is best for customers. Customers will guide technologists towards the best applications for any given technology.

Further Appreciating the Differences Between End-Users and Buyers

The actual end-user and the buyer for a product or service are often not the same, and the innovator needs to carefully consider the needs of both parties for his or her innovations and business models.

The buyer places the order and pays the bill; the user consumes or interacts with

---

1 In traditional marketing science, a survey would have these as "will definitely buy" or "are likely to buy", otherwise known as a "top two-box score," the percentage of customer voting for the two highest ratings in a range for a purchase intent question. The answers often go from "will definitely buy" to "will likely buy" to "indifferent, to "probably won't buy, to "definitely will not buy". There is typically a uniqueness of concept question also. Purchase intent and uniqueness of idea are the two biggies in quantitative concept testing.

that purchase. Each is a "customer," and each must be listened to, carefully, by the innovation team.

Consider once again the case of pet food. For pet food makers, the buyers are pet owners; the end-users are dogs and cats. Buyers include both women and men; their attitudes are different and must be understood. Most women enjoy preparing meals for their pets, mixing kibble with sauce or leftovers; for them, pets are akin to children. Most men, according to trade experts, are convenience oriented when it comes to food—the simpler the better. On the user side, dogs and cats have different nutritional requirements, and many have taste preferences. Pet food developers must appreciate both human buyer attitudes and pet requirements and tastes. And for anyone actually in the pet food business, the actual "customer" is the retail store or chain that is its direct customer. Hence, there are three important sets of needs to be understood: the retailer, the pet owner, and the pet itself.

Similar examples can be found in B2B systems and services innovations. Workers in companies use software every day that has been purchased by decision makers somewhere else in the company. Innovators in the defense sector create complex electronic warfare systems for war fighters—who care about performance in life and death situations, regardless of cost—that are procured by desk-bound program managers for whom cost and maintenance are equally important. Energy management and telecommunications systems are sold to building owners, yet the users may often be tenants.

It is essential that you determine and keep track of the precise meaning of the "customer" as you advance your Customer Value Proposition from idea to plan to reality.

Structuring Your Field Research

First, forget any preconceived notions of having a highly structured questionnaire that you learned how to create in a marketing class and might be expected to apply to hundreds of customers to get precise answers to well-known products or service features. (This comes in a later chapter when we do a "Reality Check.") It is far too early in your innovation development cycle for a large survey study.

Instead, we want you to conduct exploratory field research to ferret out a new business idea in a series of in-depth conversations with a much smaller panel of target customers. The approach of this research is called *ethnography*: direct observation and depth interviewing in the customer's place or context of use[2]. For now, we want you to work directly with customers to get your "Aha!" from the perspective of their needs and frustrations.

From this point of view, there are a series of basic questions. First, how can you identify target end-users and buyers? Who are they, *precisely*?

---

2 There are some great supplemental readings on observing users in their context of use to design innovations. See: Leonard-Barton, D., and Rayport, J. F. (1997). Spark innovation through empathic design. *Harvard Business Review*; Norman, D. (2002). *The Design of Everyday Things.* New York: Doubleday; Atkinson, P., and Hammersley, M. (2007). *Ethnography Principles and Practice*, 3rd ed. New York: Routledge.

The answer regarding with whom to speak comes from your Customers and Uses framework discussed in the prior chapter. For this phase of the process, you need to find at least a dozen or so customers in each of your target customer groups that are involved in the major use cases where you want to focus and innovate. It's as simple as that.

A Lean Design Process: What Is the Correct Number of Interviews for This Stage of the Process?

Students always worry about the number of customers to observe and converse with to get "reliable" results. Conventional marketing science tells us that a sample of a hundred or more is essential to do any serious statistics. Here, however, we are more concerned with deep insight than statistics. Deep insights rarely come from a one- or two-page survey. Instead, customer insights come from deep and thoughtful observation and conversation.

We studied a large number of "design firms"—companies that serve as innovation experts for large corporations. It showed that nearly 80% of those firms preferred in-depth interviewing with fewer than ten people for a specific design. The reason is two-fold: First, after a while, you don't learn anything new from talking to additional customers. In fact, when you stop gaining new insights is the best measure for saying "enough" rather than any hard and fast number. Second, time and money are short, particularly for the innovator. Learn what you need to learn and get on with the process of building a company. Once you launch a business and its products or services to living, breathing customers, you will learn so much more and will have to adjust accordingly[3].

For us, this the real essence and style of lean innovation: learn deeply, learn fast, design and prototype, show users your ideas, and learn some more until you achieve the design of your first, minimally viable product or service.

Talking to a hundred users and buyers doesn't strike us as terribly lean. But since you are new to this game, speaking to just six customers is probably not sufficient. A dozen to twenty high quality, in-depth conversations with customers are a reasonable goal for this stage of the process. And apart from the actual number, keep trying to speak with additional customers until you find yourself not learning anything more.

For some B2C ventures, the number may be less. For example, getting an hour with even six CIOs, or building managers, or large hospital administrators will be a challenge for most new innovators. Use your judgment, do your best, and always ask an interviewee if she or he has someone else that they think you should speak with about your innovation idea. A dozen really good, in-depth interviews with target customers are worth their weight in gold at this point in the ball game.

---

3 Meyer, M. H., and Marion, T. (2010). Innovating for effectiveness: Lessons from design firms. *Research Technology Management.* (Sep.–Oct.): 21–28.

Look for Unexpected Use Cases by People: the Case of WD-40

For example, the WD-40 household lubricant was originally just an industrial degreasing and rust-preventing spray used in aerospace applications. The company, Rocket Chemical Company, had an early industrial customer named Convair, whose engineers used WD-40 to spray the outside of its military missiles. Norm Larsen, WD-40's inventor, learned that engineers were taking the lubricant home. His own in-depth interviewing with these engineers revealed a wide range of interesting household applications. So Norm developed a new aerosol can for household use! A world-class consumer product and brand were born. In 2014, the WD-40 company approached nearly $400 million a year in sales! And it keeps coming up with innovations. Among them: all sorts of can sizes, and an aerosol straw that is built directly into the top, and new household cleaning products.

A good example came when we worked with a corporate innovation team in a large baking business. We organized a baking party at our house, inviting a half-dozen young Moms (with young children, but not present at the party). We also had a few company people—which included a chef and an R&D manager—come join in on the fun to watch, listen, and learn. The "users" and "innovators" first went shopping together in pairs. They then baked together, and afterward ate each other's cakes and cupcakes. A little beer and wine helped accelerate the conversation. The Moms discussed their attitudes, behaviors, experiences, and frustrations baking cakes. What emerged was that the Moms cared most about the frosting on the cake (as long as the cake itself was moist). They wanted a convenient way to personalize their frostings. *Easy customization* was the latent need, and it became the design driver for this corporate venture. A year later, the company brought to market several new products for frosting creations and personal cupcake decorations.

Any one can innovate this way – you, too! What do these examples mean for your projects? What sort of ethnographic experiences could you either directly participate in or construct in your dormitory or apartment? How might you do this for a pure software product or mobile application? If your venture is focused on some type of new food or drink, where can you innovate together with your target customers? Think, and then just do it.

Most Important: Work With Target Customers in Their Places of Use

Once you've identified target customers—end-users and buyers—how will you approach them for information and insights? We suggest the following: Do not ask them to visit you or meet in a neutral space. Instead, go to their place of activity—be it a place of leisure, of family activities, or of work, depending on your innovation idea. Half of the insights you gain will probably come from simply observing customers in the appropriate setting and seeing them respond to certain situations, rather than sitting down with them for a formal talk.

A good example came when we worked with a corporate innovation team in a large baking business. We organized a baking party at our house, inviting a half-dozen young Moms (with young children, but not present at the party). We also had a few company people—which included a chef and an R&D manager—come join in on the fun to watch, listen, and learn. The "users" and "innovators" first went shopping together in pairs. They then baked together, and afterward ate each other's cakes and cupcakes. A little beer and wine helped accelerate the conversation. The Moms discussed their attitudes, behaviors, experiences, and frustrations baking cakes. What emerged was that the Moms cared most about the frosting on the cake (as long as the cake itself was moist). They wanted a convenient way to personalize their frostings. *Easy customization* was the latent need, and it became the design driver for this corporate venture. A year later, the company brought to market several new products for frosting creations and personal cupcake decorations.

Any one can innovate this way – you, too! What do these examples mean for your projects? What sort of ethnographic experiences could you either directly participate in or construct in your dormitory or apartment? How might you do this for a pure software product or mobile application? If your innovation team is focused on some type of new food or drink, where can you innovate together with your target customers? Think, and then just do it.

The Mindset and Approach for an Effective Conversation With Target Customers

If at all possible, we want you to observe users first and talk second. Simply observing the customer's activities for an hour or so may reveal a wealth of opportunities. Your authors never cease to be amazed at the inconvenience, poor quality, or simple nonperformance users across a rich array of industries and industry sectors put up with time and time again. Seeing that, with your own eyes, will be the source of your greatest opportunity. Look for frowns, sighs, and other signs of displeasure—as well as smiles, laughs, and other signs of the opposite. Are they sitting down or on the go? Are they alone or with other people? Look for what the user is doing with other people or with other systems in their places of use. There may well be opportunities to improve teamwork or multi-person collaboration within a product or service area. And, if you are in the B2B systems domain, you will certainly have to know other systems with which your own system must work. Designing this type of interoperability up front into a solution makes life so much more convenient for the customer.

Then, it is time to talk. Once you begin a conversation, please try to listen more than you talk. You are not selling anything, yet. If you are selling anything to the customer, it is the importance of his or her needs and concerns as a user or buyer of what you want to do. And when a user tells you that something is important or a problem, always try to follow it up with, "Why is that important?" or "Why is that a problem?" This makes standard interviewing become "in-depth interviewing," a standard conversation much deeper, more meaningful, and useful for you as the innovator. Then, after the person gives you an answer to your first why, ask why again, get an answer, and ask why perhaps one more time. This gets down to the deepest drivers for a need or frustration—and if you can uncover that need, you will be able to design a solution that is indeed very powerful or come up with a marketing message that hits a hot spot.

For example, if you turn to one of your teammates for this project, ask him or her why they are getting their current degree. The first answer might be, "I want

TIP: Create an "I DUNNO" File

Any one can innovate this way – you, too! What do these examples mean for your projects? What sort of ethnographic experiences could you either directly participate in or construct in your dormitory or apartment? How might you do this for a pure software product or mobile application? If your venture is focused on some type of new food or drink, where can you innovate together with your target customers? Think, and then just do it.

Create a Word document or spreadsheet containing any questions that emerge on this project for which you don't yet have an answer. You might even want to assign a name to find out an answer to that question if you are working in a team.

Often, people forget the questions they had earlier. Then an answer comes around, but they have already forgotten the question! Too bad, because usually those questions never die—they just disappear for a while and come back to haunt people later.

Keep an "I Dunno" file of some sort. Revisit it once a week as your venture project proceeds. It will also help organize your tasks moving forward. Entrepreneurship is all about learning—for customers, competitors, solutions design, and business models—and it never stops.

to learn new things." You might then ask, "Why is that important to you?" The response might be, "I feel that without this education, I won't be able to advance to the next level in my career." You might then ask, "Why has this been a problem?" And, if your teammate has a technical background and is getting an MBA, he or she might say, "Because I was pigeon-holed as an engineer that doesn't know and cannot manage business. What a drag." The result might be an innovation-focused MBA program design that combines lots of core business management courses with innovation courses where students help their companies grow. For a different type of MBA customer, you might get a very different answer. If the student is relatively young, you might learn that the individual really doesn't know what he or she wants to do and that the MBA is a vehicle for gaining exposure to different industries and making the contacts to get a first great job in a business career. Here, work internships, as part of the MBA might be the differentiating design.[4]

This technique of asking a successive series of why's in a customer interview is called **laddering**. In your fieldwork, please try to give laddering a try. It is simple yet so very revealing.

Think about the customer's own experience with products and services in your category and how to *improve that experience*. Your mission is to discover what customers like, what customers need, and what frustrates them.

Also, come prepared. You should have an idea of the types of information that you want—information that will help you focus your product and service development,

---

4 This is a real example. At our university, this line of user research was pursued to design business programs for the older, technical crowd, and then, an internship-based co-op MBA program for younger, less experienced students. Both provide great value to each specific student customer group.

Figure 4.1
A Discussion Guide
for Conversations
With Target
Customers

1. How do you define the activity or problem? (*Teach me how I should think about the activity or problem area. It is probably bigger than how I define it now.*)

2. What do you use now in terms of products or services in this activity now? (*Teach me the current competitive set.*)

3. Where or from whom do you buy products or services? What is good about that channel? What is not so good? (*Teach me the realities of the channels or the preferred routes to market.*)

4. How satisfied are you with your current products or services that you use in this activity? What is your greatest source of dissatisfaction or frustration with using these? (Please tell me who you think is the best and the worse!) What are your workarounds? (*I would love to see them!*)

5. Who is responsible for the buying decision? Is it you or someone else? (*Can you help me speak with them also?*) How is the buying decision made? Who and what are the key influencers? (*You should be writing down notes because this is where most entrepreneurs slip up!*)

6. What are the criteria used when evaluating alternatives? Is there a clear set of metrics as part of those criteria? (*Can you teach me how you currently evaluate current products and services.*)

7. How much do you spend each month of year on products or services within this activity? (*Tell me if you think you are getting your money's worth, either by your facial expression or in words.*)

8. What would be the ideal solution for you? How would measure its value to you? (*Let me know what you think will be better than anything on the market today, and how customers would make their buying decisions.*)

9. What fears would you have in trying this solution? (*Would you ever buy something from a startup? Do you need to see a well-established brand name? Do I have to partner with a market leader in order to get you to try my wares?*)

10. Who would be the ideal supplier? What would be their approach, not just in terms of products, but in other things around the products? (*Teach me how to partner with you as opposed to just being a vendor.*)

how you price or charge, your marketing messages, and the route to market. Once again, knowing the types of information you need is different than coming into an interview thinking that you already know the answers.

Getting More Specific Insights From Your Field Research

Once you are done observing and then laddering a prospective customer to get fundamental insights, you can then pursue a more specific line of questioning to help get specific design points for your innovation. Take a look at Figure 4.1. It contains a series of questions that will provide tremendous insight into the customer if you can gain his or her confidence to share this information with you.

Please read through these questions now. Imagine what these would be like for talking to users and buyers in your target customer groups and their primary occasions of use. The italicized sentences in parentheses after each question are the types of information you want to gather.

The combination of observation, laddering, and this more detailed questioning will make you very smart about your customers—and that, dear readers, is key to success for venturing.

All this takes is some work, some open ears, and quiet time after these customer interactions to reflect on what you have learned. Sometimes this is best done with a partner, seeing and hearing customers with two sets of eyes and ears. Plus, two sets of hands for note taking are always helpful, and shared learning is always exciting and fun. And it typically takes more than just a few minutes with a customer to gain this information; you should try to get at least an hour of intensive interaction with each individual.

Often, the best way to get this concentrated interaction is simply to ask the user if you can join him or her in your targeted use case—such as when the user is shopping, exercising, cooking, working, using or fixing machines, or searching for certain types of information on the Web. You can ask the questions in Figure 3.1 as you join him or her in this activity.

When it comes to the detailed interview questions shown in Figure 4.1, it is very important for you to remember to:

- Position and conduct these discussions as *conversations*, not formal interviews. The customer is the teacher, and you are the student. This means detaching yourself from the solution for the moment—even if you are the smartest person in the room and think you know five times more than the person with whom you are speaking.

- Use *open-ended* questions—that is, questions that cannot be answered with "yes" or "no." You can see that none of the questions in Figure 3.1 can be answered "yes" or "no."

- Apply the laddering technique—the *why*'s—we learned above to these questions, too.

- Note that asking the customer about his or her ideal solution only comes later, in the specific questions. You need to establish the overall context of use and the competitive environment first. Only then will the customer's ideal solution make most sense.

- Always offer genuine thanks, both before and at the end of the conversation. If you meet ten target customers, chances are that three or four of those individuals may want to participate in trying your first prototypes of a new product or service. Or, if the "customer" is a store manager, he or she might actually become a launch channel partner. In fact, treat all of these people as partners. They may help you again. *Be sure always to let them know how much you value their insights.*

Develop a Persona of the Target Customer

A "persona" is a profile of the target user, and also of the target buyer (if different). Included in that persona are the customer group's demographics, needs, attitudes, behaviors, and purchase preferences. We like to see innovation teams develop a persona for their target customers in a simple PowerPoint. Following this up with a video of the customer in his or her occasion of use is even better. Bring along that

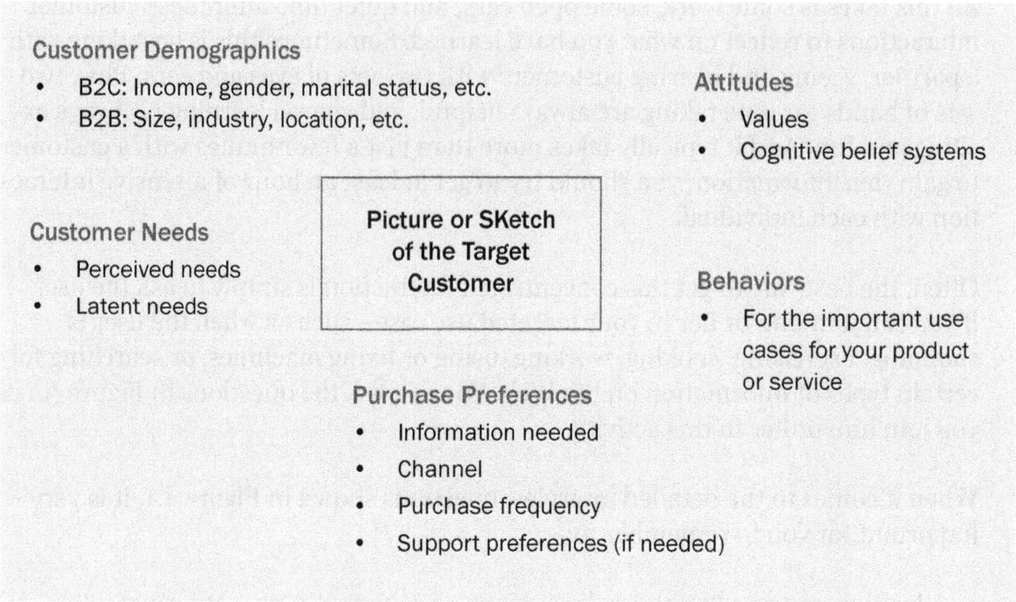

Figure 4.2
The Target
Customer Persona

Customer Demographics
- B2C: Income, gender, marital status, etc.
- B2B: Size, industry, location, etc.

Attitudes
- Values
- Cognitive belief systems

Customer Needs
- Perceived needs
- Latent needs

**Picture or SKetch
of the Target
Customer**

Behaviors
- For the important use cases for your product or service

Purchase Preferences
- Information needed
- Channel
- Purchase frequency
- Support preferences (if needed)

video-recorder on your interviews, or better yet, just use your iPhone!

Figure 4.2 shows a template for capturing information in a concise way for a customer persona. This also works just as well for a B2B customer as it does for a consumer buying a product off a retail shelf.

We define each of major areas in the Persona as follows:

- **Who they are, e.g., the consumer or industrial demographics of the target customer.** This can be age, gender, and ethnicity, or industry niche, geography, size of a company, position, and level of responsibility of the person in the company.

- **Core needs.** The customer's specific desires and frustrations as these relate to a specific occasion of use. These needs drive the features, performance, and price of a product or service. Uncovering core customer needs lies at the heart of entrepreneurial innovation. We like to think of these core needs as, in part, being derived from the attitudes and behaviors defined next.

- **Attitudes.** These are the cognitive value or belief systems of customers. An example might be a young male's attitude toward driving versus Mom driving the kids to school versus professional commuters. In a corporate setting, "you can never get fired by selecting IBM" might be the attitude of mature IT managers, whereas younger ones might prefer to go with "open systems" and use smaller, independent service suppliers to get the job done.

- **Behaviors.** These are the physical activities surrounding the use case. Using a car driving example, a young male wants to move lots of "stuff" and "party" with his buddies in his transportation; Moms and commuters display other behaviors, be it driving around with lots of kids or requiring an "office in the car" powered by communications technology. Purchasing behaviors are important here as well.

- **Purchase preferences.** Customer behavior at the place of purchase provides essential insights for consumer-focused entrepreneurs. As a simple example, it is well known that males generally do not like to shop down the aisles of a grocery store. Rather, they prefer to shop the periphery, which includes the produce, deli, and chilled (not freezer) sections of the store. An entrepreneur trying to make tasty, convenient meals for husbands who need to cook for their families needs to know this, leading to perhaps new, easy-to-prepare meal formats for the chilled section of the store. If these products get stuck in the freezer aisle, most male shoppers will never see them, regardless of need.

Also, take a picture of someone you feel is highly representative of your target customer group, and stick it right in the middle of the text containing your persona. It brings the story of your customer to life!

Within Core Needs, Look for Latent Needs and Clear Customer Frustrations

When you do your observation, laddering, and specific interviewing of target customers, realize that not all customer needs are of the same priority for the entrepreneur. Some are more important—or more strategic—than others. Here is an important approach for prioritizing needs.

There are perceived needs and latent needs. A perceived need is one that customers already recognize and, in many cases, have a fair idea of how it can be addressed: "I need it to drive faster!" "I need it to last longer!" "I need it to cost less!" Performance, quality, and price tend to be the "big three" perceived needs. All competitors in a target market segment can understand this with just a little customer research. As an entrepreneur, you must understand perceived needs as well as any competitor, but you must also do more. You need to find **latent needs**.

A latent need is a fear or frustration that the targeted customer doesn't know how to solve. The need may be expressed with a quick phrase, some type of physical expression such as a sigh or clenched fist, or even a swear word. Part of that frustration is that the customer knows of this problem but *doesn't know how to solve it*[5]. Then later, when you present that same customer with a solution to the problem, he or she says, "Great! That's perfect!" You have put a smile on your customer's face, and hopefully, obtained a customer for a very long time.

One the secret weapons of successful entrepreneurs is that they work hard to find and validate latent needs in their target customer group for very specific use cases. They have then built great businesses based on providing clear solutions for those latent needs, with a form, function, and price that screamed "value" to the user. This can be your recipe for success as well.

This is the path to success: to truly differentiate yourself and your offerings, you must discover customers' latent needs and build solutions for them into your products or services—or how much you charge for these offerings. If you can find

---

5 Meyer, M. H. (2007). The Fast Path to Corporate Growth. New York: Oxford University Press.

one or two latent needs and address them clearly and well, you will be on the path to success.

At the same time, you must also address perceived needs that the customer expects in any product or service. Consider this the price of entering an existing product or service category. For example, Tesla electric cars get tremendous acceleration, have great suspensions, and boast comfortable, luxurious interiors— all in addition to being electric vehicles with a 200-mile to 300-mile range on full charges. Teslas meet both sets of needs for the affluent but energy-conscious customer.

Latent needs are often found in the following areas:

- **Safety.** This latent need is driving entire industries, including border and facility security systems. Many of these ventures are spin-offs from large defense contractors. At the consumer level, the Spot Satellite Messenger (www.findmespot.com) is designed for outdoor adventurers, allowing them to send emergency locator beacons from any place in the world directly to emergency response teams and loved ones.

- **Reuse.** Reuse is a growing concern and source of frustration in industries. In software, it has become a major play of market leaders such as IBM (with its Services Oriented Architecture and associated software tools). In consumer products, it is transforming manufacturers' approaches to packaging volume and materials.

- **Sustainability.** This is a major latent need, particularly among younger customers and the industries that serve them. Once consumers have finished using

Figure 4.3
3 Examples of Perceived and Latent Needs

	Perceived needs	Latent needs/frustrations
For a product	I want the best tasting, smooth chocolate that I can buy for $20 a box	I love chocolate but I know all the sugar makes me feel fat. I wish I had a great tasting, indulgent chocolate that was also low fat.
For a system	I want my CAD software package to connect to the new generation of 3D composite material printers so I can quickly produce prototypes	All my engineers make individual CAD drawing on their computers, but nothing allows them to make sure they share common components. There isn't any reuse across our product lines and it's loisng us a lot of profit
For a service	I want to get my MBA online because I don't have time to sit in class	I took an online class but I never got to know my professor or any of my students. I could have just read the books. I didn't learn anything from my classmates.

Example: Latent Needs in the Classroom

When you do your observation, laddering, and specific interviewing of target customers, realize that not all customer needs are of the same priority for the entrepreneur. Some are more important—or more strategic—than others. Here is an important approach for prioritizing needs.

What are the latent needs among yourselves as users (e.g., students!)? Well, one of them must certainly be collaborative learning. You read from a book and write notes in your notepad or on your computer. You do the same for class lectures. The professor shares his or her PowerPoints with you on Blackboard or by e-mail. Then there are the supplemental readings. And you meet with classmates to share your notes either for project work or exams. When it comes time to study or advance a term project, you must gather all these different pieces, integrate them, and move forward. Everything is "point to point" rather than a seamless, integrated portfolio of knowledge, learning, and sharing. And it all "goes away" after the semester is finished.

Where is the software venture that is seeking to integrate this entire classroom experience into a mobile, collaborative, lasting experience, erasing the boundaries between textbooks, notes, group work, and presentations, and replacing them with authorized sharing between teachers and students. While we are all stuck with Blackboard, who is trying to disrupt this category so near and dear to all of our hearts? There must someone! We've run across a few in Europe and several in the U.S., but no one has hit a homerun yet. Maybe it will be you!

Make finding a latent need and solving it a litmus test for developing your venture idea. It is the best way to ensure that you won't have a "me-too" product or service.

Figure 4.3 provides examples of customer statements for perceived and latent needs. Before proceeding forward, take a moment to read these statements. Make sure you understand the difference between a perceived and latent need. Then jot down some notes on what you might expect to find for perceived and latent needs among your target customers.

a product, they are increasingly frustrated that they have to throw the product or packaging in a garbage bin. In many U.S. cities and towns, for example, one must pay a $20 fee to dispose of an old refrigerator, air conditioner, TV set, or computer monitor. Some ventures have flourished by recycling used equipment or replenishing equipment (e.g., inkjet and laser printer cartridge refills). We have watched another student venture, Pure Pest Management, grow to provide environmentally safe, organic pesticides to residential and commercial properties. Sustainability is a powerful driver for entrepreneurship and innovation.

- **Personalization.** In a world of mass-produced products and services, many customers appreciate—and will pay extra for—items tailored to their specific needs. Few suppliers know how to address this need. Those that do can differentiate themselves. Dell rose from obscurity, in part, thanks to its ability to use flexible manufacturing to customize and quickly deliver PCs.

- **Convenience.** It seems that the Web is a particularly good venue for ventures that strive to make shopping and delivery convenient for consumers. Even without the Web, many service providers are now trying to provide their services any place, any time, and anywhere.

Any one of these types of latent needs can be a powerful driver for your own innovations. Also, products and services that address latent needs are less subject to price discounting—at least, during the early stages of market penetration.

Make finding a latent need and solving it a litmus test for developing your innovation idea. It is the best way to ensure that you won't have a "me-too" product or service.

Figure 4.3 provides examples of customer statements for perceived and latent needs. Before proceeding forward, take a moment to read these statements. Make sure you understand the difference between a perceived and latent need. Then jot down some notes on what you might expect to find for perceived and latent needs among your target customers.

Look at the Before, the During, and the After of Each Use Case

Identifying specific use cases is really important for innovation.

For example:

- **Products:** Gifting chocolate. Giving your girlfriend chocolate for Valentine's Day is a specific use case for which you might want specific flavors, colors, and even (for you guys) a "rush service" because you only remembered Valentine's Day a few days before! There might be a different use case for your wedding someday—where you want to buy hundreds of dollars of special, customized chocolates with your bride's picture on the packaging or on the chocolates themselves. Or, for Mother's Day.

- **Systems:** Medical equipment. Monitoring patients has different use cases for monitoring in the hospital, monitoring in the home, or monitoring "on the go," e.g., an ambulance.

- **Services:** Financial planning. Financial services planners love use cases: for example, saving money for your child's education is a different use case, featuring different approaches and financial products than saving for your own retirement.

Use cases involve the element of time. This provides a use case with a really interesting structure: *before the primary use, during the use,* and *after the use.* And though "during" might be the main event for competitors in your category, you can uncover powerful latent needs in the *before* and *after* as well.

For example, an amateur astronomer takes his equipment to a backyard viewing location, aligns the telescope's mounting with the celestial pole, and sets out his star charts, red flashlight, and other accessories. He may also have to drag out a

TIP: Lead User Innovation

Wouldn't it be great if one of your target customers has already designed the solution you want to sell?! In fact, history has shown that the early forms of successful commercial innovations can sometimes be found right in the hands of customers in a target industry niche. With careful observation and good discussion, you might well find those lead users. They face a problem, but rather than sit on their hands waiting for a solution, they create their own solutions. Yet they don't really want to leave their companies to commercialize their inventions. That's where you might engage.

long electrical extension cord. This may take ten minutes, and it occurs before any stargazing activity can begin. The *during* phase involves finding the desired celestial objects in the sky, which may involve some calculations and searching, examining them under different magnifications and with different light filters, and perhaps some photography. The *after* part of this astronomer's use case involves bringing in and storing his equipment, logging his observations in a notebook, and possibly working with digital images created during viewing.

It's easy to be so fixated on the *during* part of a customer's use case that the *before* and *after* parts get overlooked—though each may be equally important for the customer and serve as the basis of a differentiated product or service solution. Using our backyard astronomer's experience as an example, equipment makers have been highly innovative in making the *during* activity easy and enjoyable. A

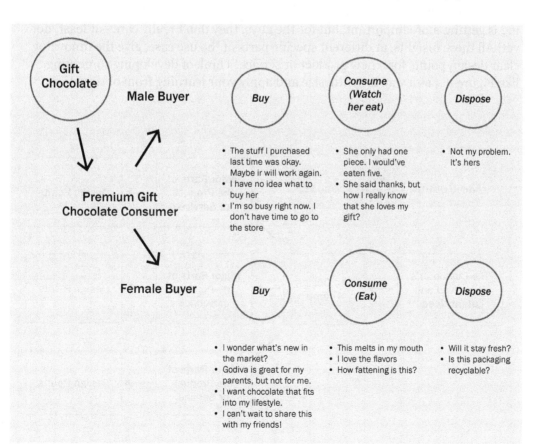

Figure 4.4
Use Cases: Perceived and Latent Needs for a Gift Chocolate Venture

new generation of computer-guided telescopes point directly to a deep-sky object selected by the user from a handheld menu, eliminating the need to work with charts, make calculations, and fumble around in the dark. The before is served by download maps of the universe for specific observation; and the *after* with recording and note taking through mobile apps delivered with new telescopes.

Let's return to chocolate gifting for a simple yet revealing example. Take a look at Figure 4.4. This is the result of a team's field research with consumers of premium gift chocolate. Figure 4.4 also represents a template to guide your own work for the before, during, and after parts of a customer's use case. The Figure shows two use cases: one of the male buying for his female partner and the other of the female buying for herself and her friends. As you observe customers in their places of use, capture specific phrases that express their needs at each point in the use case. For perceived needs, use a regular font. For those needs that you feel are latent (unsolved frustrations), use an italic font to set them apart.

In the example, the team found the obvious: Men and women are completely different "animals" when it comes to chocolate! They have different motivations, different worries, and different needs in (a) buying chocolate, (b) eating it or watching it being eaten, and (c) disposing of the packaging.

The statements in Figure 4.4 are not only humorous but revealing. For the guys, "I am so busy right now; I don't have time to go to the store" suggests an occasion-specific eCommerce solution. Or for the women, "I want chocolate that fits into my lifestyle" might mean youthful, contemporary packaging with upbeat colors and candy combinations. For young professional women, recyclable packaging is getting more important, but for the guys, they don't really care—at least, not yet! All these insights, at different specific parts of the use case, give the innovator clear design points for a new product or service. Think of developing something like Figure 4.4 as a way to synthesize and apply your learning from observation,

Figure 4.5
Drive User Needs into Design Themes, and Then into Specific Features in Your Product or Service

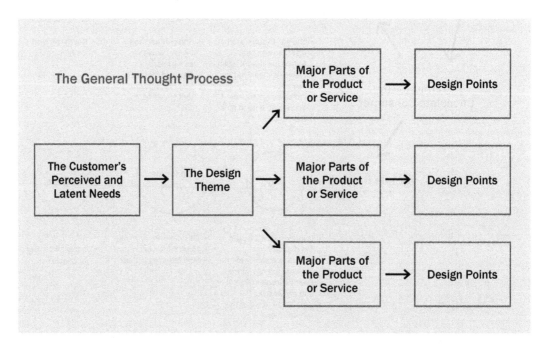

laddering, and the detailed questioning described earlier in this chapter.

Creating the Product or Service Concept

With target customer insights in hand—the problems and needs of a specific set of customers for a specific use case—the next step is to translate your idea into an initial product or service concept, or a combination of products and services.

This is the really creative part of the innovation process. You have done a lot of thinking to get to this point. Remember, you want to be highly focused on a target customer and use. Also, when you create a product or service idea, you want it to be distinctive, not just a me-too idea like others already on the market. To make it distinctive at this point of the process, the best thing to do is to make your initial product or service idea directly address the "latent needs" you uncovered in your user research. Innovators score by leveraging latent needs into new solutions. At the same time, your product or service still has to meet the industry standard for satisfying the "perceived needs" of customers.

Figure 4.5 shows an approach for making sure that your product or service is distinctive from a user's perspective. It has four basic parts:

- The customer needs

- The design theme for your product or service that your think emerges from those customer needs

- The major components or parts of your product or service (some people would call this the high-level architecture or the major subsystems)

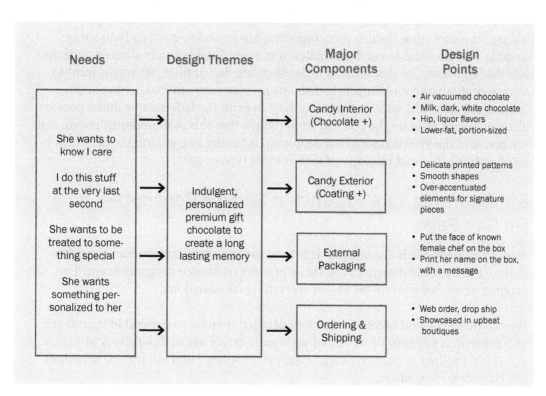

Figure 4.6
Designing a Product
for Men Buying
Premium Chocolate
for Ladies

TIP: Breaking Tensions is Another Way to Think About Innovation

Another way to think about latent needs is as "tensions" among target customers. A high-performance car that gets out-of-sight fuel economy solves a tension; a wonderfully casting fishing rod that is ultraportable solves another in the mind of a fisherman. Great-tasting but healthy food is a never-ending example, as are highly portable medical devices for monitoring that can save people's lives. "I want to use powerful medical technology, but I can't carry it on my belt or wear it on my wrist": Tensions such as these are gold for the entrepreneur if he or she can create a solution. Customers will say, "I can't believe they are doing that . . . all that work is for me! What a great product [or service]! What a great company!" When you can make something possible that, in the customer's eyes, had not been possible before, your venture is poised for success.

Then, as the figure shows, you first want to create design themes that address your customers' major needs, frustrations, and problems.

Figure 4.6 continues with the chocolate gifting example, an upscale gift chocolate venture aimed at young professional men as buyers, and their ladies as the users. All the classic emotion, convenience, and personalization needs are listed on the left of that Figure. An indulgent personalized gift to create lasting memory is the design theme. Then we have the major parts of the product—the interior of the candy, the exterior shell, and the packaging—as well as the ordering and delivery service. Keep it very high level and simple at this stage of the process. Then we show a list of features that apply specifically to each part of the product. These include sucking all the air out of the chocolate so that it feels ultra-smooth and creamy in the mouth; buying high-quality chocolate of different basic types; and having "middles" that feature contemporary, hip liqueurs—such as Daiquiri or Tequila Sunrise—and lower-fat, smaller, more permissible candy sizes or portions. For the "signature" pieces, such as little chocolate fish or mice, we might want to over-accentuate the molding of the fish lips or mice ears—to make these items "pop." And we might want to figure out how to print the lady's name and a personalized message right on the box—to let her know that this is something special, just for her. And the Web ordering and drop-ship is for the last-second buyer, which is most certainly the vast majority of men for this type of gift!

Summarizing Your Product or Service Concept — On One Page

Now we come to the home stretch. It is time to formalize your product or service design. Professional designers call this a product or service design concept. The product or service concept builds on everything we have done.

We call this a concept because it is more detailed than just a general idea, and yet, as a concept, it needs to be validated with some target users. Take a look at Figure 4.7. It is a Product or Service Design Concept template filled out for our premium gift chocolate idea, where:

Customer Needs, Benefits Sought Customer = Gen Y/X Male	Implementation Design Points
• Create a lasting memory of emotion/ love • Indulgence, good taste, a treat • Contemporary, modern, youthful • Sustainability in a clear way	**Product or Service Features** • Indulgent taste with dark, rich chocolate • Fine cocoa butters • Liquors and other premium fillings • Contemporary top design patterns • Smallish portion sizes for women
	Packaging Features (if a consumer product) • Made from recycled materials • Soft pastel colors • Contemporary graphics suggesting premium gifts
	Channel and Merchandizing Strategy • End-cap in premium retailers, • Or Point-of-sale display for holiday seasons • Online store with drop ship for personalization
	Messaging and Web/Social Strategy • Godiva is for your Mother; this is for you. • Fair trade is really important, and we are it • Donate % to sustainable cocoa growing co-ops

Figure 4.7
The Product/Service Design Concept

- **The target customer** is a professional male and the use case is a Valentine's Day gift, a special one at that!

- **The needs sought.** Based on our prior research and discussion, the target male buyer wants to create a lasting memory, indulgence in the taste and design, and a social, sustainable quality in the product or package.

- **Product features.** In this case, we have small-portioned chocolates, dark fine chocolate, liquors and other special "middles", and Fair Trade origins.

- **Package features.** Soft pastel colors, recyclable, a "heritage" design, and perhaps even personalized messaging on the box, such as "Forever …"

- **Channel/Merchandizing strategy:** this is how a product is sold, and where it is sold. For our chocolate concept, it would be primarily in high-end retailers, such as Neiman Marcus, in a special store-in-store display, or to achieve personalization, through the Web and drop-shipped to the person receiving the gift.

- **Messaging and Social Strategy:** highlighting the functional, emotional, and social benefits. For the chocolate idea, it might be a "loving, tasty gift, pleasing to the eye, pallet, and the environment."

This template needs should be followed up with a sketch or mockup of the product or service concept itself. Figure 4.8 shows an example, borrowing from one of America's best known chocolate chefs – and our own favorite – Jacques Torres.

Anticipating and then validating customer benefits is so very important for the entrepreneur because it is the basis of competitive differentiation. You can think of benefits as being purely functional (the chocolate tastes better, or the car accelerates faster), emotional (the chocolate makes her feel special, or the car, makes the older guy feel younger), or social (the chocolate is Fair Trade in origin, or the car, really *Green*.) Think about the benefits of your new product or service in a multidimensional way. Understanding different benefits for your target customers becomes the basis of building a dynamic brand (which we will cover in Chapter 6).

It still surprises us just how many bright, young entrepreneurs fail to look at their solutions from a clear customer-benefit perspective. Whether it's from arrogance or even just laziness, it is often a fatal flaw. It is not what you think about your products or services that matters; it is what your *target customers* think. And that has been the point of this chapter. Now go apply the methods, and have fun doing it!

Where We Go Next

In completing this chapter, you have come a long way on the road to creating a successful innovation. You now have much more than an "idea." You have a product or service concept, based on the needs, fears, and frustrations of your target customers for their important use cases. Hopefully, your innovations can make a big difference in their experiences during these use cases, and that is why the processes described in this chapter are generally known as "experienced-based design." You should be excited, if not totally pumped!

In the next chapter, we will learn how to take a product or service concept and transform it into a full-fledged product line and suite of services. No entrepreneurially thinking innovator makes money on a "onesie." But first, do the Exercises right below, and then we will take the next step. And, if during your customer research, you come up against a barrier – such as no clear opportunity to improve on current solutions – do not be afraid to pivot to another use case or another phase of the current use case. If anything, good innovators are flexible; they keep pivoting until they hit a great solution and then a business model for it.

READER EXERCISES

You have done industry analysis by this point in your project. You have also hopefully had that breakfast or lunch with a seasoned businessperson from your target industry. Now it is time to take your research to the next level. The only way to truly understand customer needs—and therefore the solutions you need to create and sell—is to enter the realm of the target customer.

Step 1: Hit the Streets and Talk to Customers in Their Use Cases

Your field work for this chapter is to observe and talk to target customers. That might be just two or three users at this stage, or it might be six or seven. No need at this point to talk to a lot more: We want quality more than quantity.

Figure 4.9
Customer Interview Guide

1. How do you define the activity or problem? (*Teach me how I should think about the activity or problem area. It is probably bigger than how I define it now.*)

2. What do you use now in terms of products or services in this activity now? (*Teach me the current competitive set.*)

3. Where or from whom do you buy products or services? What is good about that channel? What is not so good? (*Teach me the realities of the channels or the preferred routes to market.*)

4. How satisfied are you with your current products or services that you use in this activity? What is your greatest source of dissatisfaction or frustration with using these? (Please tell me who you think is the best and the worse!) What are your workarounds? (*I would love to see them!*)

5. Who is responsible for the buying decision? Is it you or someone else? (*Can you help me speak with them also?*) How is the buying decision made? Who and what are the key influencers? (*You should be writing down notes because this is where most entrepreneurs slip up!*)

6. What are the criteria used when evaluating alternatives? Is there a clear set of metrics as part of those criteria? (*Can you teach me how you currently evaluate current products and services.*)

7. How much do you spend each month of year on products or services within this activity? (*Tell me if you think you are getting your money's worth, either by your facial expression or in words.*)

8. What would be the ideal solution for you? How would measure its value to you? (*Let me know what you think will be better than anything on the market today, and how customers would make their buying decisions.*)

9. What fears would you have in trying this solution? (*Would you ever buy something from a startup? Do you need to see a well-established brand name? Do I have to partner with a market leader in order to get you to try my wares?*)

10. Who would be the ideal supplier? What would be their approach, not just in terms of products, but in other things around the products? (*Teach me how to partner with you as opposed to just being a vendor.*)

We also want you to spend some serious time observing and talking to target users in their own place of use and place of purchase. If it's dog food, that means visiting their kitchen while they're feeding their dogs or accompanying them on a shopping trip to PetSmart, for example. If it's premium chocolate, that means visiting chocolate boutiques or coffee shops that sell premium chocolate, perhaps forming a small focus group with your friends. (Here, you might split up the men from the women so that each can talk freely!) If it's software, that means going into companies to spend time with the end-users of your type of software, or a few doctors or nurses for medical software, or a few architects and building owners at the buildings themselves for energy management software. Use Figure 4.9 as your discussion guide. And don't forget to "ladder" your interviewees!

Spending time in the field with customers is what the most successful innovators do—their inspiration comes from users. Remember, this is a difference between invention and innovation. Invention is a brilliant engineer or scientist sitting alone in a lab creating new technology or basic science. Very few inventors create category-leading companies. Innovation, on the other hand, is the application of known technology or science to solve consumer, industrial, or social problems. Innovators learn what to do from end-users and then work to figure out the hows. Successful entrepreneurs then take the matter one step further, transforming those users into paying customers.

The discussion should go well beyond product or service issues. The marketing and business model insights it seeks to gain from customers are the foundation of designing a powerful, dynamic venture strategy. We are confident that if you follow the discussion guide in your conversations with prospective customers, you will come back with new insights and inspiration. While this is "serious" work, it is also the most fun an innovative entrepreneur can have other than the joy of experiencing a multimillion-dollar "exit" seven or so years down the road.

Step 2: Create a Persona for the Target Customer

How well do you really know your target customer? Prove it by developing a profile of that customer by completing the template shown in Figure 4.10. Surround a picture of the representative target customer with key phrases that pinpoint:

Figure 4.10
The Customer
Persona Template

Customer Demographics
- B2C: Income, gender, marital status, etc.
- B2B: Size, industry, location, etc.

Attitudes
- Values
- Cognitive belief systems

Customer Needs
- Perceived needs
- Latent needs

Picture or SKetch
of the Target
Customer

Behaviors
- For the important use cases for your product or service

Purchase Preferences
- Information needed
- Channel
- Purchase frequency
- Support preferences (if needed)

- Demographics, including income, gender, marital status, etc., for consumers; size, industry, etc., for B2B

- Core needs, latent as well as perceived

- Attitudes, cognitive values, and belief systems

- Behaviors in the important use cases for your product or service

- Purchase preferences in terms of information needed to make a purchase decision, channel, purchase frequency, and getting support (if needed)

Step 3: Develop Use Cases with Perceived and Latent Needs

You should come back from your field interviews with notes, perhaps videos, and fresh memories. The next step is to develop the primary use cases that will be the focus of your venture. We saw how this worked for the premium chocolate team.

Now it is your turn to create this for your venture idea. To do this, use the template shown in Figure 4.11. Don't forget to try to incorporate the before, during, and after for your primary use case(s). And then try to distinguish between perceived and latent needs—for example, needs that customers expect all competitors to solve, and others that are pure, maddening frustrations that they aren't sure anyone can solve!

Step 4: Develop the Product or Service Concept

Lastly, construct your product or service concept. That's the template shown in Figure 4.11. Go to work! Make something truly special—something that you think your target customers

Figure 4.11
Customer Use Cases
Template

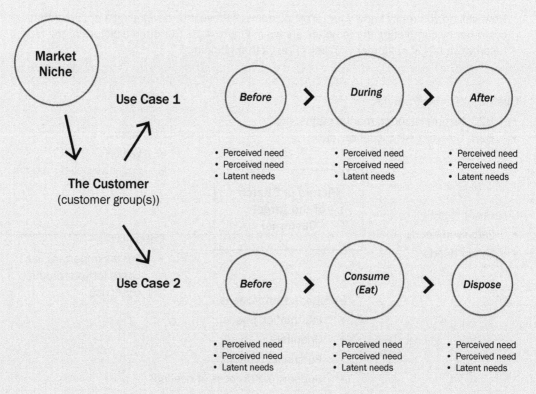

will truly appreciate and enjoy. Focus on improving the overall experience of the user in his or her use case. Remember our discussion about design themes, and how to drive these into certain parts of the product, the package, or the service. All the while, think about the functional, emotional, and social benefits of your design concept – the things that will make it different and special in the eyes of target customers.

Put your findings into a short PowerPoint. This should be another major checkpoint with your teammates, your professors, and your classmates. Show everyone your product or service concept. Explain how it relates directly back to your target customers, their use cases, and their needs and problems within those use cases. Remember the importance of latent needs as well as perceived needs, and where you are focusing in terms of the before, during, and after within the use case. And definitely *draw or sketch a picture of the product you want to create*. If it a service, sketch the use case you are addressing, with perhaps an "As Is" and "To Be" representation of the use case improving with your innovation.

Perhaps most important, bring your customer interviews into the conversation as the evidence for your choices. The insights from those conversations should make you confident about your work. But at the same time, *listen to the feedback* and think. And as you hear comments or criticisms, place yourself once again *into the hearts and minds of the target customers* to filter what you are hearing and how you respond.

Customer Needs, Benefits Sought Customer = (Short description)	Implementation Design Points
• • • •	**Product or Service Features** • • •
	Packaging Features (if a consumer product) • • •
	Channel and Merchandizing Strategy • • •
	Messaging and Web/Social Strategy • • •

Figure 4.12
The Product or Service Concept

DESIGNING AND PROTOTYPING THE MVP

5

The Purpose of the Chapter

Now that you have develop a new product or service concept, and a product or service strategy around it, is time to get more specific and do a more detailed design, and then, some rapid prototyping so that you can begin to show successive versions to target customers – improving your designs to reach an MVP (minimally viable product or service) needed for commercial launch or deployment as a service.

Achieving Elegance in the Design of New Products and Services

Customers recognize elegance in design when they see or use a product or a new service. For a product, its appearance is pleasing and in keeping with its function. It is easy to use and serves its purpose without complication. If it has user controls, their purposes and operations are readily apparent and self-instructive. Form and function have a seamless unity. In The Psychology of Everyday Things, Donald A. Norman explains, well-designed objects are easy to interpret and understand whereas poorly designed objects can be difficult and frustrating to use, preventing the normal process of interpretation and understanding.

Engineers also recognize design elegance, but at a deeper level, focusing on inner as well as outer qualities: the appropriateness of the materials, the economy of components, and the ease with which they fit and work together. Manufacturing managers, too, know design elegance when they see a design that requires a minimum number of parts and assembly steps. If the product is a piece of software, engineers look for user interfaces that are intuitive, making sure that simple tasks are easy to do as well as allowing users to readily perform more difficult tasks.

Services designers also value elegance – greatly. A new, innovative process actually simplifies complexity while at the same time delivering greater value to the user. Increasingly computers, sensors, and other forms of technology are being used to streamline and automate complex processes.

In sum, well-designed products and services achieve elegance in both form and function. They are efficacious: they do what they are supposed to do, and appear to the user to do so with ease. Just think Apple, whether it's computers, its software, or its on-line or retail store environments. If you like cars, and very much depending on your persona as a car buyer, you are definitely going to love one of the new BMW, or a Prius if you are another type of user, or the new Miata if you are yet another. Each of these designs provides a distinctive synthesis of form and function for its intended target user. While everyone may not be a fan, Uber definitely rings this author's buttons with its easy to use, price advantage, and driver rating, all through mobile technology.

Elegantly designed products and services don't simply happen by chance. They are the outcome of a process starts with **storyboarding**, is followed next with methods for **composite design**, and last, by fast-cycle prototyping of those designs to give users something they can more concretely respond – and help you design something even better. Today, people like to call the fast-cycle prototyping and review process, **agile development**.

Think Beyond Engineering
When Designing A New Product or Service

Make no mistake – the products or services we feel best about are not only those which not only function best, but which also provide a clear emotional connection with us as users. This connection emerges when you substantially improve the user's overall experience in the use case with your new product or service.

For example, your author likes the Mazda Miata not just because it zips around traffic so very well, but also because of its exterior and interior styling or packaging. I not only enjoy driving a Miata, I like being seen in one as well. Other types of target users feel the same way about their BMW's (high performance) or their Land Rovers (outdoor active). My Miata solution gives me a sense of freedom and self-enjoyment, at a price that I find reasonable. My colleague's BMW does the same for him. In this sense, our vehicles are more than just transportation on four wheels; each is its own experience and hence, allows us as users to form an emotional connection.

The innovator must dig deep into his or her ethnography to find those points where an emotional connection can be forged. Part of this is the aesthetic or appearance of the product or service, supported by the brand name and messaging around the innovation itself. Another part is the manner in which the innovation improves the user's overall experience by performing functions in a clearly better way than existing products or services, from the user's perspective.

Through your understanding of target users in prior work of this handbook, you should now know their fears and frustrations through total use cases. Conceiving

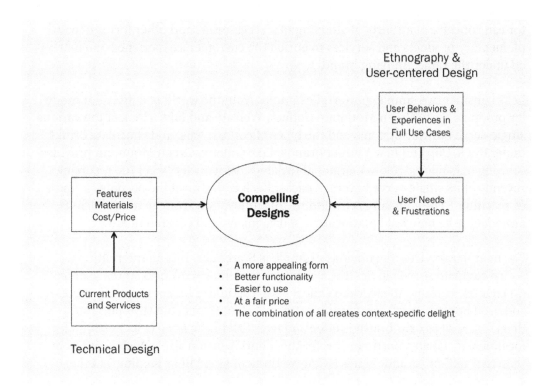

Figure 5.1
Synthesize Engineering Considerations with User-Centered. Experience Design

of product and service designs that relieve these frustrations and tensions, or eliminate them altogether, is hugely important.

Form and function blend together to make an innovation that is compelling to the user. Take a look at Figure 5.1 and ask, "How does this thinking – the synthesis of form and function – apply to the innovation I wish to create?" In the side column of this page, take a moment right now to list the two or three ways you think you can transform your product or service innovation into something that users not only like, but also will cherish, smile a bit when using, and then enthusiastically recommend to others.

Next, Think Like a Good Engineer about the Modularity in the Design of New Products and Services

The engineered design of a product or service is also hugely important. And when it comes to good engineered design, we think about modularity. A modular design within a set of products or services is like Lego: Different parts or components can be assembled together to make the final product or service for the customer. For example, a modular design for a food product might be if a manufacturer could replace sugar and other carbohydrates with lower-calorie ingredients to provide two types of snacks, regular and diet. Or, in software, a company could provide a base-level product, such as Microsoft Word or Excel, for which users "plug in" various templates and macros to provide specialized functionality. Or, in services, a company could send out skilled service technicians, like Best Buy's Geek Squad, who apply specific rules and procedures for different appliances and media systems for installation or repair.

Why is modularity important for the innovator? Modularity helps you create new streams of revenue by easily serving closely related sets of customers. The innovator can conceive of all sorts of attachments, accessories, and other forms of complementary products and services to enrich the customer's experience—all marketed under the same, unifying brand.

Let's consider two simple, powerful examples from the world of coffee. For modular products, go to Green Mountain Coffee's Website and take a look at the various single-serve brewing systems and the types of coffees, teas, and chocolate drinks under the K-Cup and new Vue subbrands. Like Gillette, Green Mountain provides brewing machines at a low-margin, affordable cost in order to get the recurring revenue of its single-serve beverage packs. Each coffee machine becomes a "money machine"! The company is extending this innovation strategy to cold drinks, announcing its new Kold platform for sodas, juices, and cocktail mixes.

For modular services, the obvious example is Starbucks. It is an international coffee company, based in Seattle, Washington, with over 20,000 stores in about 60 countries around the world. While it sells a standard line of premium espresso-based hot (espresso, cappuccino, latte, macchiato) and cold (frappuccino) drinks, as well as drip-brewed coffee and teas, Starbucks adjusts its portfolio for localities. In Japan, consumers prefer the "short" portion size, which is different than the "tall" or "grande" sizes (what we think of as small or medium) in the

United States. Japanese customers also love teas, and Starbucks in Japan has a fantastic drink called "matcha frappe"—made from finely milled green tea, ice, and a little cream. And in terms of retail store layout, the sit-down store layout is different than an airport retail layout. Starbucks even has a partnership with cruise ship operators for Starbucks onboard.

If these two great companies can create modular designs for their products and services, so can you. It is one of the fundamental enablers for successful innovations. But it takes some careful thought about the design of your products and services.

Let's Get Started: Storyboard Your Innovations for Major Use Cases

We really enjoy visiting Delft Technical University in the Netherlands, and in particular, it's School of Industrial Design Engineering. At any given moment, there are hundreds of students from around the world designing new products and services for companies seeking fresh insights into old or new problems. The pin-up boards and flipcharts are often covered with three specific types of charts: personas (which already know how to create from our prior chapter), storyboards of new products and concepts during major use cases, and a series of alternative concept sketches such as the front, side, and rear view of a car. In this section, let's learn storyboarding. It is simple, fun, and powerful.

A storyboard, in the design context here, is a visual representation of how a new product or service concept takes form, appears, changes, and transforms in its use the target use case. A storyboard brings an innovation concept to life. It is

Figure 5.2
Storyboarding a Product or Service in Use. An Example of a Mobile App for Finding a Place to Park on Campus

incredibly important for your, as an innovator, to take this step of visualization and activation for your idea.

Take a look at Figure 5.2 as an example. It shows the storyboard for a campus student safety network. Some readers might call this type of storyboard a wireframe for the mobile app. The user (typically a female student) has a small dongle, which connects through Bluetooth to her cell phone. Pressing the dongle button for a sustained amount of time alerts the campus police to the person at risk and her GPS location. The dongle can also be used to signal friends in non-emergency situations on their respective locations. The different use cases are shown in the wireframe, both for campus police (the map) and the student (the cell phone images.)[1]

Sometimes we find it useful for process intensive innovation to do an "*As Is*" and "*To Be*" storyboards, where the after is an improved process based on the innovation. For example, for a wearable wireless glucose monitor, the *As Is* storyboard might show how a diabetes event is either poorly managed, and then, the *To Be* storyboard a well-managed situation through a series sketches of the user and mobile app screen images that show the alerts, the patient's interaction, and the response by health care professionals if needed.

Or let's take a traditional service – such as finding an apartment in a new city. Let's say that our innovation is a mobile app to help international students find an apartment in Boston with .5 miles of their favorite type of highly rated ethnic restaurants and other amenities, combining rental apartment availability for brokerage databases with local restaurant databases and so forth. Our intention is to have students use the app before arriving in Boston to get a jump on other students showing up on campus for the first time. And if possible, to use social preferences to match prospective roommates with current apartment leaseholders in search of a roommate.

The *As Is* storyboard for the use case would show the new student trying to figure things out directly with brokers the week before school, and then learning about nearby amenities after the fact. The *To Be* storyboard would show a set of screen shots app would literally show a bunch of screenshots of the app through the entire use case. For example, the first screen shot might show a search screen the area within Boston (this could obviously be any city), the number of rooms requested and price range, access to public transportation, and perhaps with a little algorithm that estimates trip time to the student's new school. The next screen would then show restaurant choice preference (as in Open Table). There would then follow screen shot of apartments in range and nearby restaurants, with the ability in subsequent screen shots for a virtual tour through a specific apartment, and the a few pictures of the food and the menu from nearby preferred restaurants. A following screenshot would then make an appointment to speak with the local broker, and another perhaps, to provide a coupon for eating at the student's new preferred local restaurant. Brokerage commissions, restaurant advertising placement, and some percentage of the first coupon redeemed might be the venture's business model.

---

1 Our thanks to Abby Titcomb, founder of Knightly, a smart safety network, a venture in the Northeastern University student-led incubator, IDEA.

If you have the time, take a minute or two to draw a storyboard for getting a taxi on a busy city street during rush hour. Then storyboard Uber. Do you see the elegance in Uber's process design? What perceived and latent needs does it solve for both passengers and drivers?

Next, take a minute or two right now to sketch a storyboard that make sense for your product or service innovation. Don't try to make the storyboard perfect yet. Just outline the major steps as the product or service is used along the way.

Create a Concept Sketch

We find that concept sketches of an actual product or the workflow of a new service are important to both sharpen and convey a team's vision for its innovation. You don't have to be a particular good sketch artist, although being a terrible one does really help the case either. If you can't draw, find a friend who can.

A concept sketch reveals a team's design vision for its innovation. For example, Starbucks had the design vision of a retro café. Such design visions drive functional considerations – such as the types of "handcrafted" drinks brewed at Starbucks – and form considerations – where the cafes themselves feature wood, warm pastel colors, and lounge chairs as well as tables.

Design sketches often started extreme or somewhat radical, and then get watered down in the realities of product development. Figure 5.3 shows the concept sketch made by Honda designers for a new SUV concept, called the Model X. It was

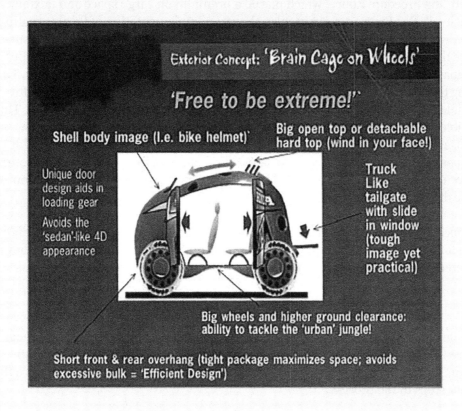

Figure 5.3
A Concept Sketch for the Model X: The Brain Cage on Wheels

Reproduced with permission of Honda Motor Company

Figure 5.4
A Concept Sketch for the Model X: The Freedom Zone

Reproduced with permission of Honda Motor Company

commercialized as an SUV called the Element, one of the company's first cross-over vehicle designs. The original concept sketch was very hip and quite extreme, titled "a brain cage on wheels." Note the large wheels, the funky styling (compared to Honda's CR-V for example), and the nontraditional central pillarless, open swinging doors (perfect for hauling gear or partying at the beach.) These features cost Honda a lot more money to tool on the manufacturing floor but to its credit, Honda stayed true to the vision that emerged from is user-centered design efforts.

The team also developed a different concept sketch for the interior of the Model X, titled "the Freedom Zone," which placed a premium on cargo space and flexibility in using it. See Figure 5.4, which also shows an implementation of flexible seating. The design center for Honda was located in Southern California, and it is no surprise that the design team took its inspiration for the interior concept from a beach lifeguard station, where young men and woman store all sorts of various gear. To bring the interior concept to life, Honda's engineers created a new paradigm for flexible seating (the ability to fold seating any which way desired by the user). The flexible seating paradigm has worked its way into many other Honda vehicles. This, along with a no-carpet hose-it-down interior, and a pop able moon-roof at the posterior (to carry bookshelves on other tall items during apartment move-in/move-out) became the hallmarks of this rather unique vehicle targeting the young male driver.

A concept sketch for a mobile app can simply be the storyboard we described above. And for a pure service innovation, the best concept sketch is a workflow that shows different types of user and providers interacting at different steps of the process.

Composite Design for Products and Services

The next step for bringing innovation concepts to life is to create more of an engineered design for your new product or service. We call this a "composite design" of product or service subsystems that seeks to optimize overall function. Here are the major steps in the process:

1. **Develop a product or service architecture.** Developing a composite design requires that your first define the architecture of the new product or service, which means identifying the major subsystems or parts of the product or service, and if appropriate, the way they are connected, e.g. the interfaces between the subsystems. From a design perspective, the overall aesthetic or appearance of the total system is an important component for physical products or software that has a human interface or GUI. This aesthetic or styling should be considered its own special subsystem. And for consumer packaged goods, please do not forget the package. Make it a separate subsystem, too.

2. **Explore different options for implementing each major subsystem.** For a chair, for example, we might define the architecture as having a seat, feet, a back support, arm rests, height and depth positioning subsystems, plus the overall appearance or aesthetic. Then, for the frame, we might consider metal, plastic, composite, or wood as possible implementations. And vinyl, woven materials, or leather for the seating and back panel, different types of tilt mechanisms, with or without synchronization, and optional lumbar support mechanism. All of these options have price and performance implications relative to the users and competitive offerings.

3. **Select the options for each major system that you believe will make for the best overall product design for your target customer and market.** In the chair example, we might select a composite frame, a mesh back for breathability, seat height and depth adjustment, coordinated seat and back tilt mechanisms, a multi-position lock with position memory, lumbar support, foot rollers, and all with a very pleasing, contemporary design – for the premium $800 plus office market segment. The process of assembling preferred options for specific subsystems into an overall design is what we refer to as a composite design simply because different elements are brought together.

4. **Perform a competitive assessment of the composite design for function.** The composite design is then assessed for function against its known competitors already in the market. Innovators tend to either ant the overall design to be superior to existing products or services in some clear way, or to be dramatically lower cost. Not all subsystems need to be superior to achieve a premium offering – just a few, while others can remain at parity with competitors. And aesthetics can also be a differentiating factor or subsystem. In a car, for example, the exterior styling is itself a major subsystem, just as much as the interior comfort subsystem, the driver controls, the chassis, and the powertrain.

5. **Perform a competitive assessment of the composite design for cost.** This is where you need to sharpen your pencils – or spreadsheets. The selection of materials dramatically affects manufactured cost, using plastic for example, instead of wood. While most students will not have specific cost information for each specific subsystem, try to make a relative assessment against current competitive offerings (e.g. less, the same, more on a per unit basis).

6. **Map the composite design along a performance-price spectrum against major competitors' products or services.** Is the design the best performing and the most expensive for customers in the target market? Or, does it only perform at

Figure 5.5
A Structured Design
Bubble Chart: A Gift
Chocolate Example

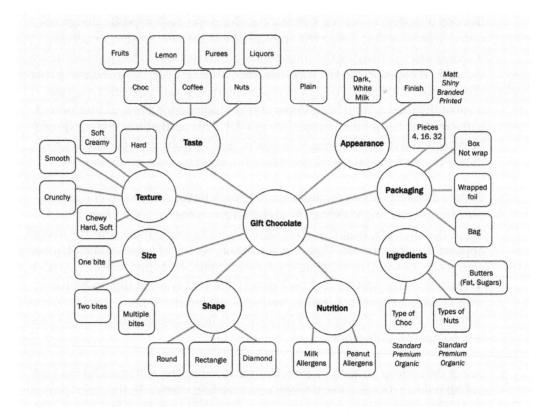

parity with most other products or services, but differentiates strongly on cost? Or (and the positioning we prefer), is a price-performance leader, deliver great and competitive differentiated value to the customer while being clever is the design so as to take out certain costs – the classic "more bang for you buck" approach.

7. Integrate and compare to competitive products or services. You then step back, look at your composite design and assess how it might fare against current competitive offerings in the target market in terms of performance and price. Hopefully, have arrived at a superior function at equivalent or lesser cost relative to rival solutions. And for a physical product or user interface for software, an aesthetic or appearance that should be highly appealing to your target customer based on their attitudes, behaviors, and preferences for style, simplicity, and convenience. In some cases, innovators can charge more than current competitive offerings if their offer superior functionality. Even if you can't charge more, superior functionality at price parity with competitors is a good way to penetrate the market.

Figures 5.5 and 5.6 show two methods for incorporating the seven steps above into a composite design – for a physical product. These two figures carry forward the gift chocolate example from the prior chapter. We call Figure 5.5 a bubble-chart for structured engineering design. In the center is the overall product concept, Gift Chocolate. Surround it are the major subsystems from a design perspective: Taste, Texture, Size, Shape, Nutrition, and Core Recipe. Appearance is that styling subsystem mentioned above. And, you can also see that Packaging is included as its own major subsystem.

Subsystem	Performance Leader (s)	Our Composite Design
Taste	Fran's Chocolates; Vosges Haut Chocolate; L.A. Burdick; Lindt Excellence	Superior, amongst the best, with unique flavors and spices
Texture	Ferraro Collections	At parity
Size	Mars (for value, Dove Chocolate)	At parity
Shape	Ferraro	At parity
Appearance	Jacque Torres, Mr. Chocolate; Vosges Haut Chocolates	Superior, competing with Torres
Packaging	L.A. Burdick (as but one example)	Better, although play up sustainable packaging
Core recipe ingredients	Green & Blacks Organic Chocolate	Superior, organic, fair trade chocolate
Our Product		*Superior in Taste, Appearance, and Core recipe ingredients, better than average with sustainable packaging, but at parity in texture, size, and shape. It will be priced at a premium.*

Figure 5.6
Assessing the Performance of a Composite Design Relative to Competitors

Then, for each major subsystem, different possible implementations are defined. Taste, for example, has many possible options, including chocolate, coffee, nuts, fruits, and liquors. Texture in this type of product also has different options, such as soft and creamy versus hard or chewy. We can do the same type of variety for size in terms of the number of bites. Take a minute to work your away around the chart to see the logic in the specification of different implementation choices. Nutrition is an interesting one in gift chocolate – there is no formal nutrition per se, but there are allergen considerations those consumers who suffer from milk or peanut enzyme reactions. For Core Recipe, one might have regular chocolate for premium, organic chocolate, as well as different grades of nuts, butters, fat, and sugars – the choices of which will drive cost as well as taste. Also note that we could explode the bubble chart into yet another level of detail – which we would do for some subsystems in order to get really specific.

With these different options specified, you can then literally create the composite design of the product by circling or checking the options that you think fit your target customer – in this case, consumers craving a new gift chocolate. For example, we could select a variety of options for taste in a boxed chocolate gift assortment, make a few hard and creamy soft items, keep them all to a single bite, have a variety of shapes, not worry about allergens, and shoot for premium core recipe ingredients. Create a very contemporary shiny, pattern-printed exterior, and place the chocolate in a clear plastic trays in a nicely pattern cardboard boxes – and viola, we would have the premium gift chocolate offering provided by a leading chocolatier such as Jacque Torres (Mr. Chocolate) in New York City. His stuff looks fantastic and tastes even better – buttery, smooth, creamy, rich, and priced to match the premium quality. Or, we could focus on products for those with peanut allergies, have a much more limited variety of tastes and textures, skip the fancy packaging,

Figure 5.7
The Layered
Technology Diagram
for Software

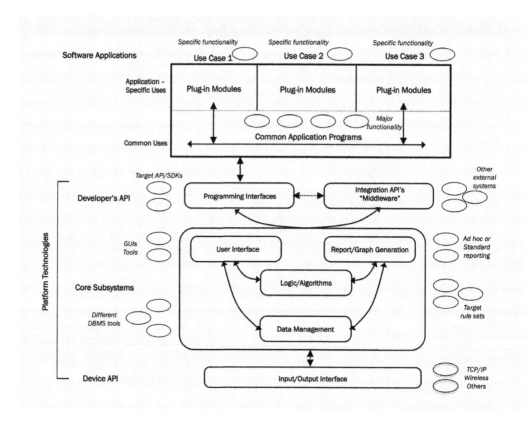

but imbue the overall design with a styling that suggest organic, clean, certified peanut-free. The composite design process is powerful and if you are making a physical product, device, or system of any type, to use the bubble chart method to scope and refine your specifications.

Figure 5.6 then shows a performance-price comparison chart, again using gift chocolate as the example. This is very important step in terms of overall subsystem integration and competitive assessment. In the figure, we show a simple table that lists the major subsystems in the first column, and then, the current performance leader in the 2nd column, and the very bottom, a performance summary of your own innovative, composite design. The last statement should also provide an assessment of the implications for price.

As the figure shows, "performance" for any given product is by no means uni-dimensional. In the case of gift chocolate, taste, texture, core recipe ingredients, and styling can all contribute to a high performance design. The figure shows the name of certain chocolate manufacturers who we consider leaders in that specific design dimension – our opinion only. Most innovators have to use their own judgment in this way, trying to assess relative position against competitors the best you can along major dimensions of performance. For the performance of a new car, for example, acceleration and economy should be relative easy and fact-based; for interior comfort, not so easy and in fact, quite subjective.

Composite Design for Software

For complex software and systems, the bubble chart approach can pretty messy simply because a software product can literally have dozens of different major subsystems. So instead, we use a different framework to represent software product architecture that is a layered technology diagram. That framework centers on a layering or hierarchy of the components of many if not most software systems. It is shown in Figure 5.7, a high level architecture for software applications. Admitted, it too can get pretty messy – but bear with us for a few pages to learn what composite design means for software applications.

The layering of major subsystems in Figure 5.7 starts with the data input mechanism, which for many new systems, is an automated gathering of data (particularly in the Internet of Things, or IoT). Controlling these input devices is some type of operating system, being for a computer or mobile device. Many software products do not even have the bottom layer of technology – all the input is done manually by the user. A Web app relies mostly on user input, but then again, many apps also integrate GPS location.

These data then flow into some type of database management system to be conveniently and flexibly organized for input and output. Developers commonly use some third party tool, open source or commercial, for this database layer. Above the database layer (or subsystem) is a logic subsystem which contains the internal rules or algorithms for computing, transforming, and in other ways, mining the data. Here, innovators most often tend to build their own rules and logic. This, in fact, tends to be a major part of the "secret sauce" in a new software product.

Then above this logic layer are the user interface and report generation layers of the architecture. The user interface, or GUI, can be used to interact with the system to input information and get information. The reporting subsystem is just that – for either standard or ad hoc reporting.

The next layer of technology is labeled the "developer's API". This layer is really important for software innovators. The first is an applications programing interface or library for accessing literally anyone of the major subsystems down below within the system. Most software developers want other developers to build additional applications on top of their systems – an API is the way to help make this happen. This API is sometimes called an SDK (in the Microsoft world) or just a toolkit in others.

The second major subsystem is titled "middleware." This is very important for those software systems that must be integrated with other systems in the user environment, primarily for B2B enterprise software. For example, Quicken reads in financial data from major banks and brokerage houses using a standard data format. Or, if you developing an analytics package for big companies, who will have to interface with SAP, Salesforce, or Microsoft Dynamics. This middleware subsystem includes the tools and targets for this type of systems integration.

At the top of the chart, we get into the applications space. First comes general purpose or "horizontal" applications that work for all different types of target users and for major use cases. And then above it, are special purpose plug-ins for specific users and use cases. And you if have developed and marketed a strong API lower down in the technology stack, some of these plug-ins can be made by other 3rd party developers and either sold by them, or even more interesting, through you. Note that we do not address physical delivery mechanisms in this logical architecture framework; we assume that all software will be Cloud-based, delivered over the Internet or Intranet (for inside companies) and have a mobile component of some type or another.

Once you have a higher level architecture for a software product/service expressed in this way, you can then begin building a bubble chart to express different options for each layer of the technology, as shown in Figure 5.7. Or better, just create separate pages for each layer. For example, a database can be "home grown" or a commercial database tool such as Oracle or an open systems tool such as MySQL or PostgreSQL. There are also some great tools for building Web and mobile user interfaces or GUIs, and many are free or open source. Use them, at least for rapid prototyping.

The logic module tends to be the differentiator in new software. The architecture framework will force you to consider the modules you wish to program or license into the solution. The utility of your software might be your programmed rules for a new type of Cloud-based gaming software; or a person-matching algorithm for a roommate matching service; or asset management logic to a new software product that tracks where drivers are and how fast they are driving in a fleet of delivery vehicles.

Competitive assessment on software is really a matter of functional superiority in specific areas of capability – at any given layer of the technology stack. There is no reason why a software innovator cannot develop a competitive assessment along the lines of Figure 5.6 shown earlier for the chocolate example. Your differentiation might be in your real-time data acquisition capabilities for IoT applications; the speed or flexibility of your database; or the secret sauce in your domain-specific rules and logic. Or, you may have the best programming interface in your industry, allow customers to rapidly integrate your system with their other systems. Put simply, to win at software, you must do something very new or significantly better than competitors, and at the same time, not write every single bit of code from scratch. Instead, use powerful software toolkits or databases that already exist, and preferably open source tools that area no or little cost and still high performance.

Composite Design for Services

For services redesign and innovation, we use two simple yet powerful frameworks that are shown in Figures 5.8 and 5.9. The first of these is a process innovation grid, be it for an externally facing service or an internal process within an existing organization. The way to use the framework is to list the major steps or activities within the service or process down along the first column of the Figure. These are the equivalent of the major subsystems in a physical product or piece of software. Then for each major process step:

• Identify the major problems from the user's or organization's point of view,

Subsystem	The Problem	Traditional Approach	This Innovative Approach
Ordering a Ride	• Getting a ride requires the customer to find or call a taxi. • Don't know who is going to pick you up. • Do not know an fairly precise fare for the ride in advance	• Walk to a taxi stand, and hope for an available taxi. • Call and wait, with no feedback on expected pick up time.	• The Uber App, with real-time estimation of pickup time. • Driver name, driver rating, and vehicle type provided • Good, better, best options (UberPOOL,UberX,UberXL, etc) • Provide fare estimation
Taking a Ride	• Don't know the driver, his or her track record, etc. Impersonal • Taxis are often old and dirty.	• Have a taxi fleet, maintain its quality to meet local code, but essentially invest as little as possible. • Retain taxi drivers.	• Attract any individual with driver's license and who is screen for driving record and other background checks, who is then driving their own car. • Position as a high quality concierge/livery service, where the rider knows the name of the driver, is greeted by first name. A personalized experience.
Paying for the Ride	• Don't know the driver, his or her track record, etc. Impersonal • Taxis are often old and dirty. • Desire to split a fare	• Have a taxi fleet, maintain its quality to meet local code, but essentially invest as little as possible. • Retain taxi drivers. • Cannot be readily done with credit cards	• Provide the majority of rides at a considerable discount to taxi fares. In Boston, for example, taxi fares are about 1.5X Uber fares when tipping is factored into the equation. • Cashless, using stored credit card numbers • No worry about tipping • Fare splitting is in the Uber App
The Driver for the Ride	• How to find a passenger? • For most, the driver needs to make a considerable up front or weekly investment before making any money; or pay the call center for passengers. • Handling credit cards and tipping • Dealing with cash • Risk management in terms of not knowing the customer	• Wait in line in taxi line or stand, or get a call from the taxi call center • Charge a weekly fee in order to drive a cab • Take credit cards or cash • The customer may provide a good tip • Nameless customers. A security barrier separates driver and passenger.	• 80/20 revenue split • No up front or weekly fees for drivers • Uber app provides best driver routes • Uber provides identity of driver rating of the passenger
Providing Feedback for the Ride	• Driver performance • Passenger attitude	• No information on driver record or passenger attitude provided.	• Multi-sided driver and rider ratings.

Figure 5.8
The Services/ Process Innovation Grid: Illustrated with Workplace Insurance

thinking back to what we learned about perceived and latent needs. If you can identify a major frustration or latent need for a process step, that's great because it becomes a design driver for innovating the process.

- Develop a few phrases or bullet points on how these problems are current addressed by the service or process providers.

- Thinking hard and creatively, propose a few phrases that capture how you wish to innovate and address these problems. In many instances, innovators are using information technology, analytics, and workflow automation to both clean and speed up inefficient and error prone processes.

- Last, what are data and metrics that might be used to measure the effectiveness and efficiency of improvements to a particular process step? We also try to do this for the overall service or process.

Just like designing a new product, you do not have to create a totally innovative approach for every major process step – just for the one or two that you feel will make a substantial improve the user experience. The others can be at parity with the way others are providing the service or process now.

Figure 5.8 is actually illustrated with an example of that we have created for crowdsourced, ride on demand transportation, e.g. Uber. Uber is such a wonderful example because nearly all of us have tried it by now and can appreciate the innovations created at different key steps in the process. For example, for the process step of finding "a ride," the user would have to either call a taxi company or go to taxi stop, not knowing for sure if taxis would be in line and available. Uber

Figure 5.9
The Process Flow
Map: Illustrated with
Uber

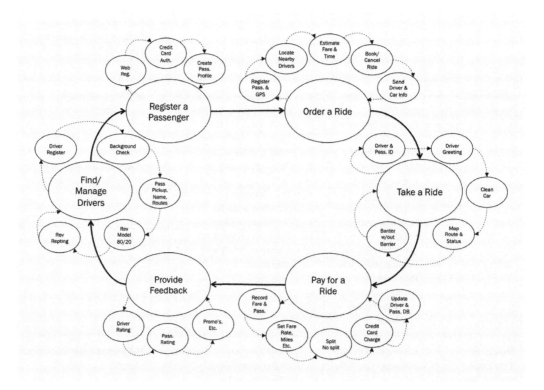

pioneered a different, innovative approach: the user download's an app, pinpoints his or her exact location, can see how long it will take for a pickup, and then order the ride. The user can then actually see the Uber driver working his or her way to the pickup, and they can call one another if they cannot find one another. Plus, the experience is personalized because first names of the driver and rider are provided, complete with prior user or driver ratings. This is so much better that the impersonal and often unfriendly encounters in traditional taxis.

You can see in Figure 5.8 that we list other major process subsystems, each with interesting innovations for the rider and the driver. For the finding drivers, Uber screens any individual with a valid driver's license, and if accepted, provides them with a special Uber iPhone loaded with various capabilities. This is a second job for many, and a primary job for others who are tired of having to pay a taxi company nearly a thousand dollars a month in some cities to simply rent a car before making any profit. For the ride itself, drivers come up with their own, typically very clean vehicles, as opposed to the typical dirty, shabby, and poorly maintained taxi. For the fare subsystem, these are set by Uber itself – and not a municipality – with the further innovations of peak, off-peak, car-pooling, and premium pricing tears. We have found the fares with Uber often half the price relative to taxi's in the city of Boston. For the payment subsystem, the rider pays through his or her credit card – and not to the driver, but through Uber – and from the user's perspective, no hassle of tipping. It is cashless and in developing countries where credit card theft is common, very secure. Plus, Uber has implemented a "split the fare" capability – really hard to do in a traditional taxi unless one is paying cash. Then, for the driver payment subsystem, profits are split 80% to the driver, 20% to Uber. In fact, the drivers I have ridden with have told me they earn more than when they were traditional taxi drivers, even without tipping, and not upfront investment or hassle other than fueling their vehicles and keeping them clean. For the rider, Uber is more convenient, less expensive, cleaner, and friendlier than a traditional taxi. And for the driver, more money, more sense of ownership and autonomy, and elevating a menial job into one of personalizing a service. Uber is not perfect, but no service is perfect. Nonetheless, is as a robust an example of services design and innovation as any we know.

Take a look at Uber's own design Website to get a feel for how the company implements its own form of the principles in this workbook. (uber.com/design) Yes, Uber is facing a host of law suits from the politicians and established interests around traditional taxi services – but it is a marvelous example of services innovation.

Next, we turn to more specific process design. Look at Figure 5.9, which is a process flow map that then gets into the details of services design. It complements the prior Figure. You can make these process diagrams as simple or complex as you like. A good storyboard from the prior section of this chapter will drive these process maps towards completeness.

Now think about how these two frameworks to a major process that you suffer through as a student on campus. Many students complain about the roommate selection process or finding living quarters, particularly if they are from overseas and are visiting the city/campus for the first or second time. Others students regularly complain about the lack of variety and cost of campus food, and don't have the

Figure 5.10
Prototype and Test:
Illustrated with
Healthy Pet Snacks

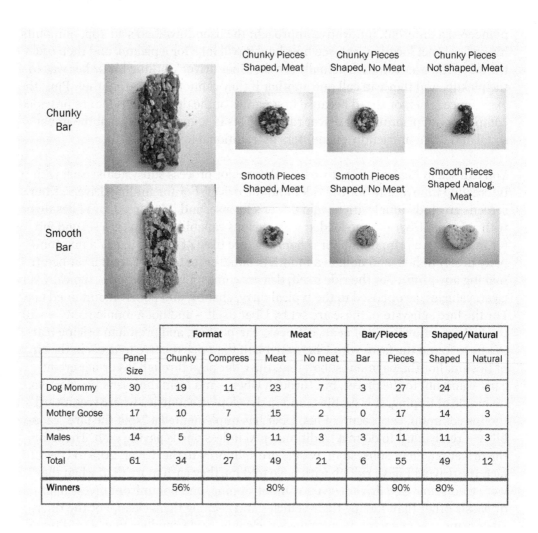

		Format		Meat		Bar/Pieces		Shaped/Natural	
	Panel Size	Chunky	Compress	Meat	No meat	Bar	Pieces	Shaped	Natural
Dog Mommy	30	19	11	23	7	3	27	24	6
Mother Goose	17	10	7	15	2	0	17	14	3
Males	14	5	9	11	3	3	11	11	3
Total	61	34	27	49	21	6	55	49	12
Winners		56%		80%			90%	80%	

time to venture off campus during the busy school week. What might be solutions to these or other problems that you, as a user, suffer from on a regular basis?

Onwards to Prototyping the New Product or Service

This is where the rubber meets the road. Put your ideas to form. You have your overall sketch of the product or service. Now, start drawing some of the major parts of components with the product. Think about how this design matches up against the "persona" of the target user—the type of user, be it a consumer or a person within a business, and their needs, frustrations, and behaviors. From the drawings, you might then try:

- If it is a food or drink product, go back to your kitchen, buy the ingredients, and prove your worth! Bring samples to class. If you are a software hacker, wear the badge proudly and go build a simple prototype of the user interface and some base-level functionality of the mobile app or software system you wish to create. Bring the product portfolio to life as simply and cleverly as you can.

- For other types of products, make cardboard or paper components or shapes for either the product or the packaging of the product.

- If appropriate for your types of products, go to the store and acquire similar types of products that have features and packaging that you think would work well for your proposed product. Also, try to get examples of "good, better, best" that have worked in your industry. You don't have to buy all these products; often, simply doing a Web search will provide you with all the images you require for a PowerPoint that can accompany your prototype.

- Use a software tool, such as Visio or even a CAD tool, to further design the product. If your university has a "3D" printer, you can even create a small-scale prototype for your product.

Lean or "agile" development is clearly a preferred approach. This means making a series of prototypes, showing them to users, getting feedback, and improving your prototypes. Then repeat the cycle. Usually three or so cycles get you to the design of an MVP.

Figure 5.10 shows a series of prototypes made for a line of health dog snacks. The questions going into the innovation project were where consumers wanted a bar format or pieces, and if pieces, shaped pieces or non-shaped pieces. A chunky versus smooth appearance was another question, as was also meat versus no meat (vegetarian). The team developed four distinct personas based on gender and age. It then went to an industrial kitchen and baked a number of recipes using different types of ingredients and showed them to a number of consumers over the weekend in a dog park. (These prototypes were not fed to any dog. Further sterilization would be required to do this type of consumption testing.) The consumers looked at the prototypes and voted for their favorite designs. The winner was: Chunky, Pieces, Shaped, and Meat. The composite design and testing gave the team a clear direction.

There is a wide range of services that allow a startup team to design, source, manufacture, and test new product concepts. Some innovators we know have found www.guru.com a useful source for finding just about any type of type of engineer, from software to mechanical engineering. Or you can upload your product designs on www.mfg.com. Coroflot (www.coroflot.com) or iFreelance (www.iFreelance.com) are also good sites to explore for design and manufacturing partners. Then there are services that use 3D printers to quickly produce prototypes from CAD software models. These prototypes can be used for rapid feedback on design efficacy and from target customers. Another option, for small-scale, plastic-injected molded products, is Protomold (www.protomold.com).

If it's a software product, software tools are so powerful and flexible now that in the hands of a skilled programmer, a basic prototype to show customers can be developed in a matter days or weeks. Look for those open source tools!

For services, prototyping simply means working with prospective users to walk through a process design. Get their reactions; look for the amount of time and effort it saves them receiving the service. How is your innovation helping them to solve a current problem or frustration? Model the customer's use case as a structured workflow and seek ways to streamline it. In this way, you can make their life or work more convenient and better within that use case. At the same time, you will see what type of information technology you require to provide and measure the results of that service. The bottom line is that to prototype services innovations, you need to roll up your sleeves, walk into the kitchen, and get your hands dirty—except that kitchen will be in the customer's place of work or leisure, depending on the focus of your team.

Prototyping means low cost, rapid, iterative, and fun! Don't go overboard. Is there a fellow student, a small design firm, or a customer engineering firm that, for little money, can help you create a prototype, be it a mobile app, a consumer product, or some new type of medical or electronic device? This is, of course, so industry and location specific that there are no universal answers. But do what you or your external partners can do quickly, and then show these prototypes as soon as possible to prospective users. With prototypes in hand, we guarantee that the level of interest and interaction by users will grow exponentially.

READER EXERCISES

These should be amongst the most fun reader exercises in the entire workbook.

Step 1: Storyboard

Remember that the storyboard we want you to create communicates how your new product, service, or process changes or transforms as it goes step by step through the target use case. You can use cartoons, videos, or simply descriptive text. Look at the example at the beginning of this chapter, Figure 5.2.

Step 2: : Create A Sketch Of Your Product or Service

Look at the Honda examples in this chapter and create sketches for the major externally facing elements of your product. This might be the product's appearance and the packaging for the product. If you are innovating a service or process, you are in luck – a really good storyboard is the concept sketch.

Step 3: Develop a Composite Design

Now, we get more detailed. If your innovation project is a new type of product, look at Figures 5.11 and 5.12. These are templates for a structured design bubble chart, and then, a competitive assessment your design for the major subsystems. If you innovation is new set of software, turn back to Figure 5.6 in this chapter – the layered model for software – and use it as guide. Then, also do a competitive assessment on the composite design. Apply these templates to your own project.

If you are doing a new service or business process, using Figures 5.13 and 5.14 as your guide. Go to work!

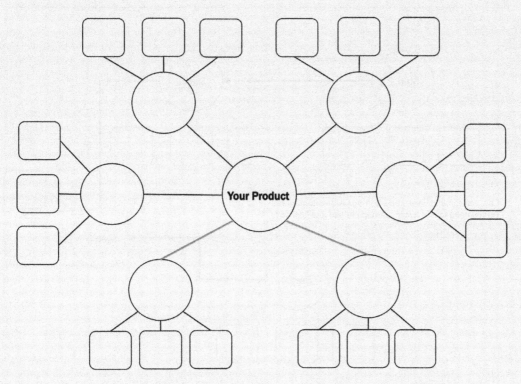

Figure 5.11
A Structured
Design Bubble
Chart Template

Figure 5.12
Assess the
Performance of
a Composite Design
Relative to
Competitors

Subsystem	Performance Leader (s)	Our Composite Design
Taste		
Texture		
Size		
Shape		
Appearance		
Packaging		
Core recipe ingredients		
Our Product		

Figure 5.13
The Services/
Process Innovation
Grid

The Process "Step"	The Problem (perceived or latent)	The Traditional Approach	Your INNOVATIVE APPROACH	Data Needed to Measure
Step 1				
Step 2				
Step 3				
Etc.				

Figure 5.14
The Process
Flow Map

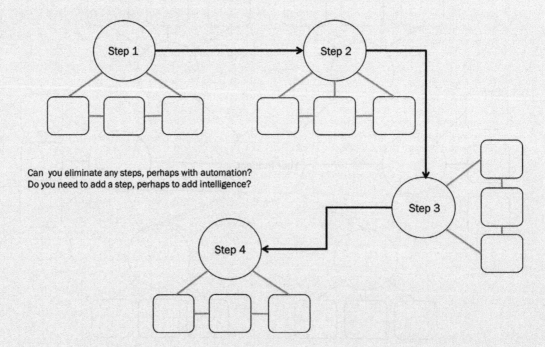

Can you eliminate any steps, perhaps with automation?
Do you need to add a step, perhaps to add intelligence?

Step 4: Develop And Begin To Implement A Prototype Development Plan

Once you have a basic design, the next step is to think about a prototype development plan that fits with the type of product or service you are creating, as well as the objective of getting something done fast and at low cost. Is it a matter of using some cardboard and glue? Or, go to your library or campus prototyping lab to use some modeling software and then a 3D printer. Who do you know that can help you do you don't have to spend two days learning the software?

If you innovation is a Mobile app, find a classmate who knows the tools and can quickly mock up a prototype or what is generally known as a "wireframe." There are a number of free Mobile app development tools available as well. One that our own students use regularly is marvelapp, which is nicely integrated with Dropbox. The entire idea is to create a prototype as quickly as possible to start showing it to prospective users for feedback.

If your innovation is a new service or process, the best way to develop an early prototype is to just start providing the service to prospective users, if possible, without any new computer programming or other sort of complexities that might be needed in the actual MVP for the service that would be required to go to market. Again, the purpose is to test the idea. If the concept is an exotic food delivery service, for example, develop a menu selected from a few local, reasonably priced restaurants, take a few orders, and go out to a local restaurants to pick up the food, deliver it, and get feedback. You can find out who wants what types of food, and when during the week. Or, let's say your idea is help dorm or apartment move-in and move-out, make some brochures for the service, get some friends for a weekend, and give it a try. See who needs it, and what you can charge. You can worry about scale-up later. For now, you just want to understand the design that will excite as well as deliver value to the target use. Remember what we learned about balancing form and function, hard benefits versus emotional appeal, and modularity in the design of things – these fundamental principles will serve you well as your bring your innovation to life.

BUILDING THE PRODUCT LINE OR SERVICES SUITE

6

The Purpose of the Chapter

In this chapter, we take the product or service concept from prior chapters and make it a more fully featured product line or suite of services. Experience shows that offering choice and variety of products and/or services to the customer—while at the same time basing them on common, underlying platforms—is essential for successful innovations in high growth businesses.

Learning Objectives

- Understand the importance of creating product lines or a suite of services

- Provide "good, better, best" in your solutions for customers

- Define technology strategies for new ventures

- Develop "lean" approaches to prototype product and service development

Defining a New Product or Services Strategy

No venture succeeds for long by selling just a "onesie." Rarely does a single product or service appeal to everyone in a target market segment with any reasonable sized industry. You need to have multiple arrows in your quiver, ready to aim and shoot for customers who believe that they have specific needs and uses beyond the standard, entry-level product or service. The old Henry Ford adage regarding the Model T—"you can have it in any color as long as it is black"—just doesn't apply anymore. Choice and variety are important for just about any target customer group, and it is up to you as the entrepreneur to define the nature and extent of that variety. And over time, variety creates new streams of revenue, important for any growing company. Just look at Google, which started off as a simple search engine making money on advertising, and which has now leveraged its databases and "eyeballs" in an ever growing range of information services.

If you are clever about it, this range of products or services can nonetheless be based on a common foundation of technologies – what we call **product platforms** – so that you can make even more profit by leveraging those shared assets across multiple products. Engineering effort can be economized and procurement of materials and components improved by buying in higher volumes[1]. Product platforms can be a common piece of software or database, a shared electrical component or subsystem, or a sauce or seasoning in foods. Platforming also applies to services. For example, a rapidly growing home repair service would want a standardized method for understanding customer needs and producing a quote for its salespersons in the field.

To do all this, the entrepreneur needs a new product or services strategy. This is a plan for developing and launching specific products or services that meet different specific needs for certain customers and target uses. The result is a product or services **portfolio**. A product line or services strategy builds directly upon the new product or service concept you created in the prior chapter, just as that product or service concept was built on the customer value proposition and all the customer research you have been performing. In this chapter, we add some flesh to the bones of the product or service concept to provide choice and variety to the target customer. And once you launch your first products, you begin to quickly learn how to refine your product or service portfolio, bringing even better offerings to your customers.

Defining a Product Portfolio With "Good, Better, Best"

An entrepreneur can ill afford to have potential customers labor over their purchase decisions. Most buying, even for business products, has an important element of impulse—induced by good branding and marketing communications, or in some cases, a darn good salesperson. Many customers tend to want to see some choices for their purchases, and find the version that they think truly meets their needs, whether it is a product or a service.

---

1 Meyer, M. H., and Lehnerd, A.P. (1997). *The Power of Product Platforms*. New York: The Free Press.

For some entrepreneurs, choice might be a selection of three or four SKUs (stock-keeping units) on a retail shelf, such as four popular flavors of healthy snacks or drinks; for others, it might be a basic software program with a growing range of "plug-in" modules that tune the software for specific uses; and for yet other entrepreneurs, it might be a core service that is, by its nature, tuned for every single customer. Just think about a successful landscaping business in your neighborhood: basic services—landscape design and planting, mowing, fertilizing, spring and fall cleanup, tree pruning—each applied in a specific way to each customer. The same applies to a successful bank. Banks are increasingly trying to customize financial services to individuals of different ages and genders.

The bottom line is that innovators – in big companies or small – do not try to force fit a single, standardized product into every customer or use case. Figuring out a simple way to provide variation, at low cost, makes the customer feel special and well served.

At the same time, the entrepreneur needs to economize on his or her efforts, especially with limited financial resources. Even a great company, such as Apple, has a confined product portfolio— even though it has the financial resources and ability to put out hundreds if not thousands of different products. Go to any Apple store and you will see only a handful of laptops, iPhones, workstations, displays, and accessories. There is choice, but constrained choice so as to keep the business simple, focused, and scalable. And importantly in the case of Apple, there is just one operating system that allows users to connect all its different devices and computers together. iOS is a beautiful product platform. And then upon it, Apple provides tremendous variety through the toils of third party developers who make and sell all sorts of apps, music, books, and videos through iTunes. Apple not only has a tremendous line up of products, but a formidable business model that has been refined and improved over time. Apple is one smart company.

Moreover, it is important to stay focused on your initial market segment and target customer in that segment. Going after another type of customer may require substantial additional R&D and time, and going after another market segment will probably require a new channel or route to market and certainly new marketing materials. Save that expansion until after you have conquered your first target market, and some solid revenue, and the experience to wisely expand into new types of applications for your technology, your products, and your services.

So provide choice, but do not go overboard with it. We recommend that venture teams initially consider just two or three different levels of functionality and price within their product or services portfolios. Those two or three levels of choice for customers can be thought of as providing "good, better, best" alternatives[2].

This way, if a customer thinks a particular offering is too expensive, you don't have to lose that customer. You can provide that person with a solution that is less costly and with less functionality. On the other hand, if the customer needs more, he or she can get it by paying more for even better products or services that your

---

2 We have lots of additional examples in Meyer, M. H. (2007). *The Fast Path to Corporate Growth*. New York: Oxford University Press.

company provides. By adding choice and variety, a "good, better, best" product line or services strategy can increase your sales by serving a broader range of people within the target customer group.

What are some examples of "good, better, best" for different types of products and services? Consider the following:

- **Products.** Go to Dell's Website and browse its computer offerings. For its desktop computers, you will see three specific subbrands: the Inspiron, for standard usage; the XPS, for high performance usage; and Alienware, with high performance graphics for gamers. This is a good example of "good, better, best," or perhaps more accurately, "good, better, different." Then, within each subbrand, Dell has the customer define specific preferences for processors, memory, disk storage, displays, and so forth. This allows customers to create "personalized" products from common components, what some have called "mass customization."[3] And only then does Dell start the final assembly process. This is followed by direct-to-consumer delivery. Imagine the inventory carrying costs if Dell had to manufacture and ship every single possible version of its computers to retailers, or if it had to carry huge stocks of premade computers in its own warehouses. Dell's customization business model transformed the entire PC industry. It also allowed Dell to bring a huge price advantage to the marketplace by bypassing the traditional retailers and their 30% to 40% markups over wholesale prices.

- **Software Products.** Many software firms offer "basic" and "premium" versions of their products. For example, one of our favorite software companies, Intuit, is a long and formidable survivor in the face of giants such as Microsoft, Oracle, or IBM. Most small businesses in North America today use Intuit's QuickBooks for their bookkeeping. Intuit used to offer Quickbooks in a good, better, best portfolio of software sold on CDs and installed on customer's machines, starting at about $300 per license for the Pro desktop version and $500 for the Premier desktop version, and an Enterprise server version that is licensed for $84 per month. But Intuit has also converted decisively to the Cloud and adopted a subscription model, featuring Quickbooks "on-line." Its Simple Start package is at $10 a month; its next level up, Essentials, is priced at $20 a month; and the high-end Plus is at $30 a month. And a sole proprietor can sneak in there for $8 a month with the Self-Employed on-line version. Intuit is another truly great company; its management, thinking hard about the product portfolio for QuickBooks, migrated to the Cloud, and developed a robust subscription model – saving itself CD production and shipment costs along the way. Go to Intuit's Website and study its offerings!

- **Services.** Computer support companies offer the equivalent of Bronze, Silver, and Platinum services featuring different levels of support. Car rental companies offer "preferred" customer plans that provide certain guarantees and expedited service. American Express's Platinum cards are associated with higher level benefits and annual fees that its Gold cards. The idea is to provide

---

3 Pine, J. (1999). *Mass Customization: the New Frontier of Business Competition*. Boston: Harvard Business School Press.

a basic service for most customers and premium offerings for customers who are willing to pay for greater richness in services. Levels of warranty are also commonly used to differentiate levels of service and are priced accordingly. Or, your variety of services might simply be tuned for specific applications or customer uses, where there is no "good, better, best," but just "different."

An IoT Example

Take a look at the example in Figure 6.1. It shows a simple framework put to good use by corporate entrepreneurs in a really large company making heavy industrial equipment – tractors, excavators, articulated trucks, and so forth. These folks had a clear vision and customer value proposition. They wanted to build IT-enabled services for their equipment, where they would install sensors on machines to measure things such as powertrain health, hydraulics, tire pressure, and even operator productivity. Each one of these measurements could be used to reduce machine operation costs, prevent equipment failures, and incentivize operators to dig, scoop, or transport more material. For construction and mining companies, the potential benefit was huge. All the machines with the sensors were to be connected through wireless networks through the Cloud to servers, where a bunch of analytics would be constantly run to detect possible problems, and otherwise help improve the productivity of the entire system, including people and machines. And after three years of development, that very system was being deployed successfully around the world.

In this case, Figure 6.1 shows how the team thought about "good, better, best" for their target customers and use cases. They first started with just trying to elim-

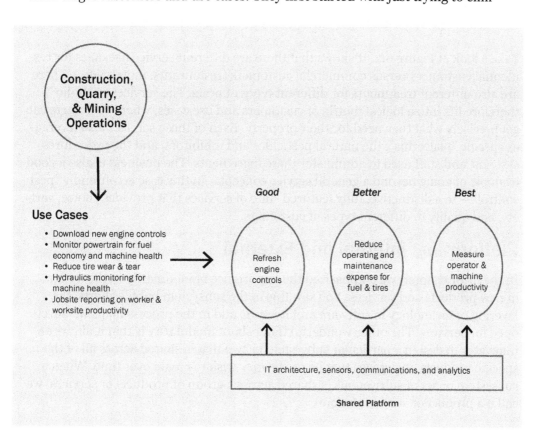

Figure 6.1
Defining a Product Portfolio for Monitoring Industrial Equipment

inate the cost of service technicians literally driving out to job sites to manually install new engine controls. That task could all be done through the airwaves with proper technology. But it became obvious that the underlying guts of the solution could be extended to monitoring powertrains and detecting impending failures. It then became clear that the same communication and analytics platform could be applied to monitoring tires, hydraulics, and even machine operators or drivers. All that was needed were different sensors, which produced different measurements, requiring different analytics. All of these new services address "latent needs" on the part of equipment owners—problems for which there were only scattered, unsystematic solutions.

The team developed its overall product portfolio strategy, but then focused first on downloading the engine controls, after that, on monitoring the engines themselves, and then on the tires, the hydraulics, and so forth. The team's company loved the strategy and then step-by-step approach for executing that strategy. The business model was to charge for each machine monitored per year.

A Traditional Services Example

We can also apply the same thinking to defining a new services portfolio.

A student venture, Pure Pest Management, developed a services portfolio based on what it considered to be "premium" pest control services for both residential and commercial applications. Its core mission was to use eco-friendly and pet-safe remedies to control mosquitoes, ticks (including deer ticks, which in New England often carry Lyme disease—a serious bacterial infection), indoor pests (rodents, ants, cockroaches, spiders, etc.), and deer themselves, which can chew up a flower or vegetable garden. All the products are plant extracts or natural oils.

Take a look at Figure 6.2. It shows that there are different service packages for residential customers versus commercial customers (restaurants, motels, etc.). There are also different treatments for different types of pests. The services portfolio therefore fits into a logical matrix of customers and use cases, where customers can get precisely what they need for their property. Each of these services also leverages specific "platforms": the natural pesticides and inhibitors, and the procedures, systems, and staff used to administer these ingredients. The business is also a good example of going beyond a general service concept – in this case eco-friendly "pest control" – to a distinctive, fully featured suite of services that provides choice, variety, and quality to different types of customers.

Platforming: Internal and External

In the prior chapter, we emphasized the importance of modularity in the design of new products and services. You saw this in the subsystem bubble charts, the layering of technology in software architecture, and in the process maps we developed for services. The other wonderful thing about modularity is that it allows an innovator to design a particular subsystem or two that is shared across all of the specific products or services that he or she may wish to create over time. When a subsystem or set of subsystems is shared across a group of products or services, we call it a product or service **platform**.

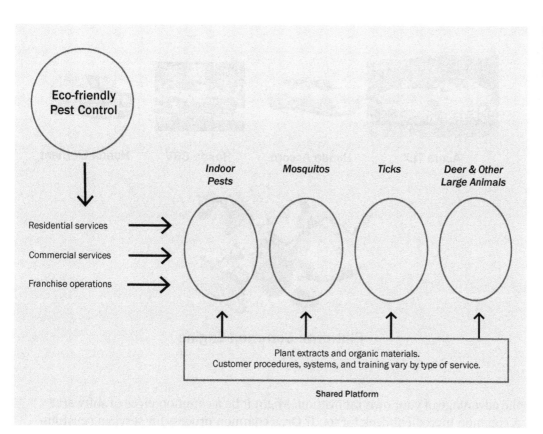

Figure 6.2
Defining a Services
Portfolio for Pest
Control Services

Product Platforming as the Core of a Product Line Strategy

A well-designed product line architecture contains an underlying platform, or perhaps even several platforms. *A platform is a subsystem or interface that is used in more than one product, system, or service.* A product platform might be an engine design used across many car models, or a library of graphic interface objects used across word processor, spreadsheet, and charting applications. The innards of your wristwatch are probably designed as a platform; its maker can offer many watch styles using that same timepiece mechanism. A platform might also be a common process, such as an underwriting process used across multiple lines of property and casualty insurance (see sidebar). The most effective platforms are those that can be leveraged across several product line architectures.

For example, Honda actually uses the same 4 cylinder engine for the Accord passenger car, its more expensive Acura TLX, and its CRV SUV, as shown in Figure 6.3[4]. This allows Honda to economize on engine components and manufacturing while extending the benefits of a long-lasting, fuel-efficient powertrain to all of these models. It also frees up resources to design and implement different versions of good, better, best for specific vehicles.

It is important to think about common product or service platforms might work to

---

4 Marc H. Meyer, *The Fast Path to Corporate Growth: Leveraging Technologies to New Market Applications.* Oxford University Press. 2007.

Figure 6.3
Product Platforms
Illustrated
with Honda

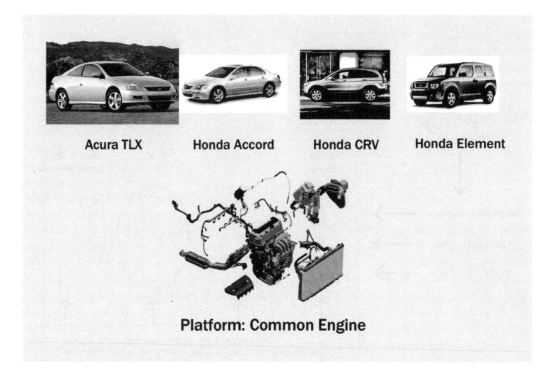

Acura TLX　　**Honda Accord**　　**Honda CRV**　　**Honda Element**

Platform: Common Engine

the advantage of your own innovation. Might it be a common piece of software? A common ingredient deck for food? Or, a common process for servicing customers, or a risk management process that can be applied to different types of financial services?

It also turns out that Honda leverages common subsystems for driver controls across its different products, as well as certain chassis designs. However, exterior and interior styling are designed uniquely to each specific product, giving different types of customers the sense that they are buying a vehicle that is truly different than others – even though the engines under the hood are nearly identical. If you do have platforming in your innovation, what are those other parts of the product architecture that will be designed differently for various types of customers. What are also the good, better, best versions of your innovation?

Externalizing Platforms an Explicit Innovation and Marketing Strategy

Some truly remarkable software companies have succeeded in making their products and technologies a platform for other companies to build their own products. Some companies have actually created a marketplace that they control to make money from other people's innovations. Think about app stores, for example. One of the best examples of this is Saleforce.com, which dominates the Customer Relationship Management (CRM) market. Salesforce.com is a set of software that allows users to track their own customers through the sales pipeline, and then, to show what products or services those customers have purchased or might we to buy. Salesforce disrupted the traditional CRM industry by being the first company to introduce a full featured, scalable Cloud based model for its software (as opposed to big client-server software). Salesforce's underlying workflow software

– its internal product platform – is called Force.com. Force.com has a set of programming interfaces that have been externalized, so that other companies can build their own Salesforce.com plug-ins, and sell these through Salesforce.com's marketplace. Today, Salesforce.com has plug-ins for many different industries, as well as analytics and other types of market tools, thanks to the army of independent software companies building applications on Force.com.

If your innovation is software intensive, use Salesforce – and Force.com – as a model and thinking about other companies innovating on top of your platform(s). Does the idea of having third party partners building products or systems on top of your own products make sense? Might this help build credibility and momentum for your innovation? What would it take, in terms of the design of your products, to make this easy for third party partners to actually do? Might it be a programming interface or software development kit? A training program for external partners? What would it take for your innovation to become an industry standard – "Intel inside," or Android?

Now, You Do It

Now, let's start thinking about how "good, better, best" applies to your innovation. Think right now about how the approach shown either in Figure 6.1 or 6.2 might apply to the basic product or service concept you created in the last chapter. Jot down some notes, for this will be a Reader Exercise at the end of the chapter. Next, think about what a platform-enabled strategy might mean for your innovation, e.g. Figure 6.3. What might be the key parts or subsystems in product, software, or service that could be leveraged across the good, best, best product or service definitions? Might any of these also become a standard for innovators to use as well, particular in the software arena?

As you do this, remember that an innovation doesn't have to have just products, or just services[5]. You can use Figure 6.1 or 6.2 to show both products and services.

For example, there are many computer "hardware" companies that now derive a majority of their revenues for selling things other than hardware, namely software and services. In fact, IBM sells even more services these days than either its hardware or software products. And within these services, IBM offers a variety of choices that include technology programming and implementation, systems integration, data center outsourcing, and even business strategy consulting.

All this is in keeping with the "whole product" idea of Geoffrey Moore, who wrote the wonderful book Crossing the Chasm, intended primarily for technology-intensive businesses. Often, the first customers of new, disruptive technology are classic early adopters— people or companies who get a thrill out of trying new things. These early adopters are willing to play around with technology. But later adopters will want more complete, mature solutions. The more your company can evolve to serve these later adopters, the higher the growth potential of your business because these later adopters tend to be the majority of the target market segment.

---

5 Meyer , M. H., and A. D. DeTore (1999). Product development for services. *Academy of Management Executive*, 10(3): 64–76.

And, customers tend to pay more for a complete solution, including services, than for just parts or pieces they have to assemble or integrate themselves. For the entrepreneur creating a B2B enterprise software company, this means you have to provide services as well as products, or at least well-engineered products that are plug-and-play for consumer markets. And sometimes, customers just might want you to outsource the whole solution for them, hosting it on a cloud.

The bottom line here is you should really be thinking about the possibilities for both products and services, not just one or the other. Later on, we will show you how to actually test customer demand for both.

A Final Thought: Innovating for Emerging Markets

Innovators are increasingly turning their attention to emerging markets given the growth of consumer and business demand in certain regions.

Many of our students—undergraduate and graduate—come from various countries around the world, and their heartfelt desire is to create a new business that will take them back to their home countries, where they believe commercial opportunity beckons. One of our students, Alvin Grayling, created one of China's first mobile (cell phone) search capabilities, based in Shanghai. One of his major customers, China Mobile, now has over a billion subscribers and is the largest mobile telecommunications company in the world. Rather than try to start his company the United States, Alvin followed his heritage and ventured into the fastest growing market in the telecommunications industry. Once there, Alvin realized that if a user's initial mobile search did not find the desired result (such as a restaurant), it was cost effective to redirect the cell phone user to a call center for human operators to complete the search. Adding low-cost call center "services" to his software "products" was essential to win a customer such as China Mobile.

In recent years, we have had students like Alvin start companies in India, Indonesia, Southeast Asia, the Middle East, and Northern Africa—literally all around the world. They all have a similar story: They want to get back home and build their own successful businesses. Yet the products or services for their home markets are not always the same in terms of performance, features, and price as those that might do well in the United States. The price-performance equation for "good, better, best" most often gets downshifted when focused on emerging markets. In fact, emerging market customers don't want hand-me-downs; they want the same performance of a Western premium product at half or two thirds the price. Getting to such a design takes innovation. Tata's Nano automobile is an Italian-designed four-seater that gets 52 miles per gallon. This sounds like a reasonable objective for any car manufacturer selling products in the United States or Europe. But for India, a car with all these features must still sell for incredibly low prices. The Nano, for example, retails for about $2,500!

The same concepts we learned earlier apply just as well here: Get into the hearts and minds of target users and buyers in these emerging markets, find out what makes them tick, and build that into your product or service concept. Then define the "good, better, best" you need for a strong product or services portfolio. More specifically, you need to think about:

- **Product design.** "The best shave a man can get" in North America, with a five-blade, super-sharp shaving system, will actually cause skin burn, ingrown hairs, and blemishes on the skin of young African males due to different skin physiologies. Products that work well in certain countries do just the opposite in others. Gerber baby foods come in different varieties in different countries: vegetable with rabbit is a favorite in Poland, while freeze-dried sardines with rice are popular in Japan.

- **Packaging.** Japanese consumers value product packaging far more than Americans typically do—it must be as stylish and appealing as the product itself. As you think about designing packaging for your own products as an innovator, consider the five senses: the impression made when you first see a product; then when you potentially hear it, touch it, or smell it; and finally, if it is food, when you taste it. Designing for the five senses is an incredibly powerful discipline—for any market.

- **Channels and Promotion.** The emerging markets innovator must learn about the subtle differences of channel partners relative to Western retailers. L'Oreal, the cosmetics giant, sells the same product in many countries, but with different promotional messages. For example, its Golden Beauty brand of sun care products is promoted to northern Europeans as a dark tanning solution, to Latin Europeans as a skin protecting solution, and to Mediterranean Europeans as a beautiful skin solution—the same product, but different perceived uses and market positioning to suit different local markets.

Recap: What We've Learned and Where We're Going

Let's recap. This is what we have learned over these past five chapters:

1. To identify an attractive market segment based on actual market data and to understand competitors and other industry dynamics in that segment.

2. To identify the different types of customers and their major use case for your types of products or services, and then to focus on a specific customer and use case for your first product or services.

3. To really get into the thinking and behaviors of these target customers—to understand their hearts and minds—so that you can drive these needs into a truly interesting new product or service design. Everything about your product or service innovation is highly tuned to improve the experience of these users, to put smiles on their faces!

4. To also focus on the needs and motivations of buyers and channel partners. A channel partner is most likely to maximize its own revenue, hopefully by selling a hot new product such as yours. But you can never take a retailer's interest in your product as a certain thing. It is hard to get onto a retailer's shelf and then, stay there. You need something really special.

5. To design specific new products and services based on your customer insights, and then, to begin prototyping an MVP.

6. To then transform that basic product or service concept into a fully featured set of products and/or services. This might include specific offerings that represent "good, better, best" for your target customers, or simply different products or services that customers require at different points in time (think about the pest control venture), or combinations of products or services for a total solution.

The purpose of these methods is to develop a clear focus for your innovation based on market realities and customer needs rather than your own wishful thinking. To complete the picture, we next need to design the business model that will accompany your products or services. *But first, a very important set of Reader Exercises.*

READER EXERCISES

Now it is time for you to build your own product or services strategy. We have created some simple templates from the examples shown in this chapter. As in prior chapters, use these templates to think about your venture.

Step 1: : Define "Good, Better, Best"

The first Reader Exercise is to apply the template shown in Figure 6.4 to define your product line or suite of services. All the customer and competitor research you have performed to date should guide your thinking here. You have segmented customers into groups, studied their use cases, and defined an interesting new product or service concept—now flex that concept into a handful of specific commercial offerings that will please different types of customers.

Remember, some customers just want the basic product or service; others will want something more advanced, and will pay more for it. Yet others will want services in addition to products; and still others who are buying primarily services will want you to include certain types of products with those services. This is about giving different types of customers what they need and want, all within your initial industry segment/niche and target customer group focus. Also, with some quick competitive research online, now is the time to begin to think about the pricing strategy that fits with your "good, better, best" portfolio design. Companies usually charge more for better and best.

After drawing your product line/services strategy, make a set of bullet points that contains the common features of your product or services portfolio. These might be a certain type of styling or packaging, a certain type of engine or microprocessor, a common user interface,

6.4
od, Better,
emplate

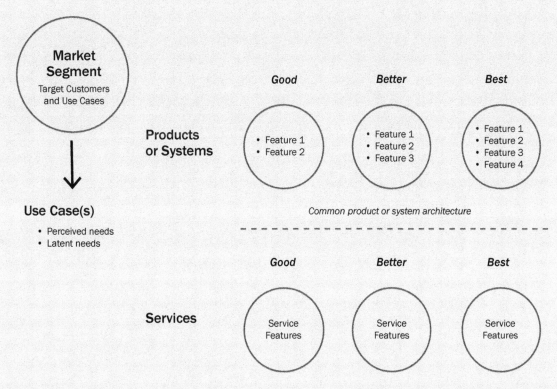

or certain service guarantees. Later on, once you are building your company, these will turn into common platforms for your products or services—things that you can leverage across the entire portfolio.

Now step back. Take a look at the result with your team members. Does the combination of products and services set the foundation for an important innovation? How can you make it even more exciting?

Step 2: : Determine If There is a Platform Play

Is there a common product subsystem or service process that can be leveraged across your entire product line or service suite – an engine underneath the hood? If one might exist, how would it have to be scaled to be suitable for good, better, best, or the more generally, the range of products and services you wish to provide.   Identify where that platform exists in your structured bubble chart, layered software diagram, or process flow map. What would have to be in that subsystem to make it a world-class driver for all your products and/or services? With Honda engines, for example, we can define the range of horsepower and/or cylinders, acceleration capability, fuel efficiency, and reliability relative to competitors. What might be the equivalent for
your innovation?

Step 3: Refine Your Customer Value Proposition

Review your Customer Value Proposition. Looks for ways to sharpen it, and other ways to improve it. From this current chapter, the very first row of the template might change or improve. (ABC is a family of products/services/solutions) that (solves which problem.)

Remember, pivoting is allowed. Adjusting your venture's focus is totally acceptable as part of the learning in your course and from this book.

DEFINING THE BUSINESS MODEL FOR AN INNOVATION

7

The Purpose of the Chapter

A great product or services portfolio means little for the innovator unless there is a clear way to make money by selling and servicing those offerings for customers.

In this chapter, you will learn how to design the business model for your innovation. You will see how a strong business model can turn a good innovation idea—the target industry niche, the target customer groups and their use cases, the product or service concept, and the product line or services strategy that fleshes out that concept—into an exciting, profitable startup or corporate venture. While we all tend to think about "innovation" in terms of new technology for new products and services, these examples show that innovating on the business model dimension of an innovation can be equally exciting and powerful. Put on your thinking cap and let's get started.

Learning Objectives

- Define what a business model is, and what it is not

- Understand different types of business models and know which ones are well suited for particular types of innovations.

- Learn how to build a business model for your own innovation and understand levers for creating robust business models, such as premium pricing and recurring revenue.

Defining a Business Model

Google, Apple, and Southwest Airlines, for example, have excellent products or services, but so do most of their competitors. Other companies sell information, sell computers and mobile devices, or sell air travel. It is the business models of these companies that have set them apart from competition, and made them industry leaders. Google slices and dices Internet and physical world data into hundreds of different offerings with advertising and other revenue models; Apple developed iTunes, using the Web to provide single songs and other media to disrupt, and soon own, the mobile media distribution; and Southwest's lean, no-frills operating model made it a leader in terms of number of passengers carried by increasing the numbers of potential consumers who thought they could now afford to fly instead of drive.

For some of you, the term business model might suggest dry finance—e.g., the financial projections for your business. That's not a business model. A business model is simply, and importantly, a) the Revenue Model for a innovation, and b) the Operating Model needed to produce that revenue.

Of course, there are all sorts of options for a Revenue Model, and, a number of things we need to consider for a detailed Operating Model, such as how we organize R&D, Production, Go-to-Market (including channels), and Customer Service.

The Customer Value Proposition drives the Revenue Model – because what and how you charge customers is directly connected to your products and services. It also drives many aspects of the Operating Model, for example, the need for R&D, the best channels for selling, and customer requirements for service.

This is shown in Figure 7.1. The Customer Value Proposition drives the business model; and the business model then drives financial outcomes and capital or money requirements to actually implement an innovation. (As a side note, if you are not familiar with any of the terms on the right side of the Figure, do yourself a favor and purchase *Financial Intelligence: A Manager's Guide for Knowing What Numbers Really Mean*, by Karen Berman and Joe Knight.)

The General Types of Business Models in Industry

There are actually many different types of "generic" types of business models across industry. Let's take a look at a few of the major ones.

- **Production/sales business model:** This model is where a company manufacturers a product and then sells it directly either to end-users or consumers, or to an intermediary such as retail store to sell to consumers. It is probably the most common and traditional type of business model – which is not to say that is old or dated. This is Apple's primary business model for its computers, with the twist thrown in that it also owns and operates its own retail stores – that are the highest revenue generating stores per square foot in the world!

- **Subscription business model:** This model is one where the customer pays either a monthly or annual fee to receive either a service, or software sold as a service.

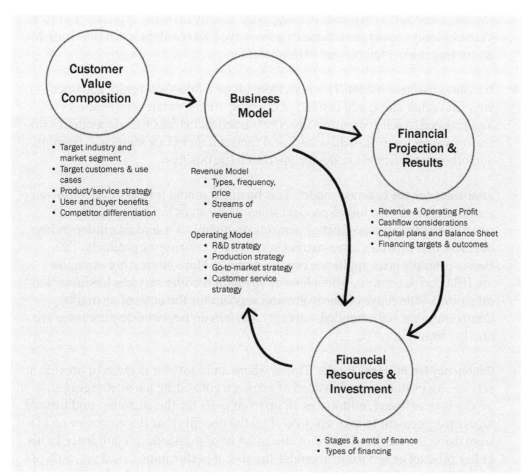

Figure 7.1
A Business Model
is the Link Between
the Customer Value
Proposition and
Financial Plans

Just think of an annual landscaping contract for your parent's home. Or, of the software powerhouse called Salesforce.com, which has taken over 50% market share by providing excellent CRM software on a per user per month fee basis, at various levels or tiers of the number of users. It has close to $6 billion in annual revenue with gross margins exceeding 65%.

- **Fee for service business model:** This model is where, for example, a consultant charges a client $500 an hour, hour after hour, for analysis and advice, or an attorney for court appearances. Or a dog walker charges $20 for a 30 minute stroll with your dog. Many consultants have a daily rate. Some business professor rockstars charge over $10,000 a day! Value is that in the eye of the beholder – often a large corporation in urgent need of strategic and operational advice. The key to success here is to be highly competent in an area of expertise – and also, to market and sell yourself as that expert.

- **Financing business model:** the financing business model is where a company makes money by buying equipment and leasing it to customers. There are hundreds of large financing companies leasing automobiles, trucks, industrial equipment, and aircraft, among other items.

- **Licensing/Royalty business model:** This business model is for inventors who have neither the desire nor capability to commercialize their innovations.

Instead, they find a corporation that pays a royalty on sales, typically 3 to 10%. There literally tens of thousands of innovative R&D companies in the United States that make their money in this manner.

- **Franchise business model:** Think McDonalds or 1-800-Got-Junk? You open your first retail store, and instead of opening others, create a franchise of it. You proceed to sell geographically constrained franchises to independent owners/operators for a "franchise fee," and then sell them raw materials, training, and other necessary elements for operating the business.

- **After-sales service business model:** This business model is to provide follow-on services, typically for initial product sales. This can either be an additional revenue stream for a product-generating company, or a separate independent business that provides after-market services for a variety of products. The classic example is an appliance repair business. More interesting examples are IBM and Accenture, which have multi-billion dollar services business that integrate a wide range of hardware and services for the enterprise market. Companies that sell extended warranty services on new vehicle purchases are another example.

- **Continency fee business model:** This is where an innovator decides to provide a service to a customer, and instead of getting a consulting fee or charging products or software, eliminates all up front costs for the customer and instead signs an agreement to take 20-30% of all the benefits that the customer enjoys from using the service. The innovator must have tremendous confidence in his or her product or service to shoulder the risk of performance. And yet, 20% of a significant cost saving in a large customer organization can lead to significant more total revenue over time.

- **Nonprofit or less profit business model:** This business model is designed to either make no operating profit or to share that profit with other stakeholders. Increasingly, social enterprises are structured to make an operating profit so as to sustain their operations, but to also constrain that profit so as to provide lower prices and other costs to consumers in need.

Understand the Winning Business Models in Your Industry

In Chapter 1, we had you develop an ecosystem map for your innovation. Time to take it out again. Identify the major players in your industry ecosystem, and not just your direct competitors. Look at the suppliers and the different middlemen sitting between you and your customers. Also look at other companies that are providing after-market products and services to your target customers.

Now, take the most successful players in these different parts of the ecosystem. What are their business models? More specifically, how do they charge for things? What are their operating models? Do they seem to be profitable from their business operations? And, what seems to be their critical area of focus – be it in R&D, manufacturing, sales, or service? And, if they are using outside suppliers, which ones? For example, are they using a certain contract manufacturer for electronics or clothes? Or, Amazon for computing power? Or, are they achieving success by selling their wares through a particular distributor or retailer?

You can often find important financial information for large companies working in your industry at Yahoo! Finance. This includes revenue growth, operating margin, operating profits, and links to annual reports and shareholder statements. In fact, a nice trick is to enter in the name of a market leader in your target industry, go to its financial information, and then hit the "Competitors" button. In a matter of seconds, Yahoo! Finance will show the size, growth rates, gross margins, and profitability of the major players in the industry. Read the news stories associated with the industry to learn more about current industry dynamics. Print out these summaries to show to your teammates. Highlight the key facts that pertain to your innovation strategy and its business model.

Take a look at Figure 7.2, which shows the business model for a premium pet snack manufacturer – a friend of ours who has local stores in the Boston area and also sells through premium retail grocers and pet shops across the country. If you ever have the chance to visit one of Rob's stores in Boston (www.polkadogbakery. com), you will see wonderfully innovative dog snacks that are designed from the dog's and pet owner's point of view. The Customer Value Proposition for the business drives the Revenue and Operating Models. Rob is a huge believer in either in-house R&D for his own snacks, or sourcing other products from other high quality

Figure 7.2
The Business Model for a Pet Snack Innovator

Customer Value Proposition

Industry / segment: Pet snacks – Dogs
Target customer: Affluent pet owners
Use case: Snacking, at home and on the go
Products/services: All natural, healthy snacks
Benefit: Enjoyment, good nutrition, dental health
Differentiation: Premium, better for pet

Business Model

Revenue model: Multiple SKU's (snacks in boxes, bags, and point of sale tins/jars

Operating model:

    R&D model: Develop in-house, in the "kitchen" in the back of the original retail store.

    Production model: Most production in the snack backing line in Boston. Other products sourced from high quality manufacturers, all U.S.

    Go-to-Market model: Our own stores first, pet specialty next, Wholefoods next.

    Customer Service model: Lots of in—store sampling, pets invited!

manufacturers, as well as in premium distribution, and a lot of sampling of new products in his own stores. Pets are welcome!

The big take-away from this story more generally is to study other people's business models just as much as their innovations. In fact, don't build your own business model until you familiarize yourself with those of other major players in your industry. This should only take an hour or two of work. And finding out how other companies make money is actually quite interesting. We want you to look at their revenue models and operating models to learn from them.

Now, Lets Work on Your Revenue Model

The Revenue Model has four basic components:

- The type of revenue (such as purchase, rent, subscribe)

- The frequency of that revenue (a one-time charge or recurring at certain intervals of time)

- The price level of that revenue (typically per unit of product or service) relative to competitors (low, medium, high)

- The number of distinct streams of revenue (such as different product lines or different services, or services that accompany products, such as paid support services for a computer). Each of these streams of revenue needs to be designed with the three dimensions above. In other words, for each stream of revenue, the type of revenue, the frequency of purchase, and the price level relative to competitors.

The design of these four components should be driven by the needs of customers, e.g. the Customer Value Proposition.

There is a fine balance between developing a revenue model that makes it easy for customers to begin doing business with your company, and giving away the store. We encourage you to try to generate a profit even on your first sales, despite all the craze for "free" or "freemium" revenue models. The idea is to create a financially healthy business.

Defining the Type(s) of Revenue

To define the type of revenue for our business, think of the type of transaction you wish to have with customers. Some of the obvious choices are:

- Is it a product that is purchased or leased?

- Is it software that is licensed or subscribed to over the Cloud?

- Is it a service that is purchased on a one-time basis only, or subscribed for an extended period of time.

TIP: When It Comes to Business Models, There Is Often More Than One Way to Skin the Cat

The same product or service concept can have two very different executions in terms of a business model. Your job is to figure out the best way.

For example, there are art innovators who have entered into the business of renting paintings and sculptures to corporations for their waiting areas, conference rooms, and offices—as opposed to selling them works of art. This preserves the client's capital, turning a capital expense into an operating expense. It also allows the client to try new art from year to year. However, this business model also requires that the art renter either purchase or lease suitable works of art.

If we enter the world of software, Microsoft or Intuit has two revenue models. One is to charge a licensing fee per server or user. The other is an annual subscription model. In software, generally, up front licensing fees are much more money than monthly or annual subscription revenue. But, then again, once users start subscribing to a service they tend to stick with it, creating a recurring revenue stream that can last a decade or more in time.

Google Apps is either free, or Google Apps for Business, a modest $50 per user per year. Red Hat offers its JBoss software development tools for $99 per year but charges thousands of dollars for its technical support service agreements. In contrast, IBM and Oracle charge tens of thousands of dollars for initial licensing fees for their own proprietary software development tools.

So consider the different options as you design the revenue model for your innovation, and let the voice of the target customer and an understanding of current competition point the way.

- Is it a mobile or Web service that you feel you need to give away, and then upsell customers in a Freemium model?

- Is it a consulting service, where you bill for time and materials?
  Or do you wish to establish and charge for an entire project fee?

- For any of the above, are you requesting cash, or accepting credit purchases?

- If you are saving the customer a certain amount of money or enabling some type of financial gain or benefit, are you extracting a certain percentage of that saving or benefit? This is a contingency revenue model.

Contingency revenue models should not be overlooked and can be a powerful method for startups that need to prove themselves to customers. For example, the Mitchell Madison Group provided forensic accounting to help large corporations reduce operating expense by reducing costs in printing, temporary labor, purchasing PCs, and renting cars and hotel rooms. Instead of charging the usual consulting day rate, Mitchell Madison established a contingency fee, taking 20% to 30% of the amount of money found and saved. Fueled by this "win-win" business model, the company grew to 900 professionals and was eventually acquired for $500 million! Mitchell Madison Group could approach a CFO of a major corporation without asking for any money up front and, even better, received payment only when the customer saved money. It was a "win-win" business model.

It should also be noted that traditional product categories (such as software) are increasingly being repositioned as services with a recurring subscription fee to the service instead of an upfront licensing fee. The benefit of services over products is that customers generally subscribe, paying month after month, year after year. Products, on the other hand, are one-time purchases. Microsoft, for example, made billions selling licenses for the Microsoft Office Suite. Now, with Office 360, it revenue model has totally changed – and in fact – has enabled it to transition to the Cloud computing environment.

Defining the Frequency of Revenue (Try to Develop Recurring Revenue)

Single, one-time purchases such a home, automobile, or boat, are obviously important parts of our economy. However, for the innovator, the one-time purchase is hardly desirable because it requires either a very expensive single product purchase or extensive reach into the market to get a large number of one-time purchases.

Instead, innovators try to design repeat purchases into their revenue model. This is also called recurring revenue. For product innovators, think about how your product can have the equivalent of cartridges for razors. And if a greater frequency of purchasing cannot be built into the product itself, think about what other products or services might complement your own products.

When a company such as Caterpillar sells a large tractor, for example, it is selling three to four tractors' worth of replacement parts over the approximately 20-year life span of that tractor. It is also now selling IT-enabled services for machine health and operator productivity. Or frequency of purchase can be increased with ongoing services sold together with single-purchased products. Think about how AppleCare has designed services to complement the purchase of a single computer or mobile device. AppleCare is a great example, as is iTunes.

Creating recurring revenue takes work. It involves producing follow-on products and services. It also includes specific marketing programs to maintain the customer's
attention. These include developing customer loyalty programs, special pricing for product or service upgrades, and other types of special promotions. An example worth considering is Harley Davidson. Its target customers, typically Baby Boomer men with average incomes of over $80,000, spend more than $20,000 on their "Hogs." But that is not the end. Replacement parts and accessories comprise about 15% of Harley-Davidson's net revenues. Apparel and other "soft" accessories contribute another 5%. The vast majority of this private-label merchandise is sourced from third parties, which means that Harley-Davidson makes no investment in manufacturing.

Every innovator should want to achieve recurring revenue from customers for an externally marketing product or service innovation. The reason is that it usually

Try to Understand the Lifetime Value of a Customer

Figure 7.3 shows a lifetime revenue model for a customer. We suggest that you take a hard look at this Figure and be sure that it makes sense to you. Lifetime value is fundamental to innovators who wish to commercialize their new products and services.

The Figure shows the various activities needed to "acquire" a customer and to start getting paid. These include lead generation, marketing communications, direct contacts with the customer, and shipping and installing the product for or by the customer.

Once the money starts flowing (the second row of the Figure), there can be a combination of the product revenue and add-on services. For a technology product, this might be installation or consulting services. There can also be revenue derived from the resale of third party products and services through your own salesforce. Supporting all of this is an ongoing set of marketing and selling programs (the third row in the Figure). Put it all together and one has a model of the lifetime value of a customer.

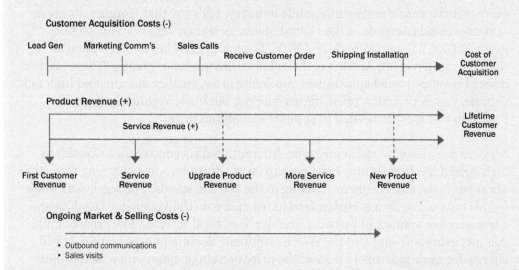

Figure 7.3
The Lifetime Value of a Customer

Over time, companies tend to improve their products and resell these to existing customers, as well as new services. These improvements cost money.

For B2B innovations, and certain Web consumer services, investors or corporate executives will want to know your projections for the lifetime value of a customer. A high number shows that you have thought how to leverage initial sales into follow-on sales, making the most from the effort to initially get a customer. For enterprise software or consulting businesses, this might be as high as $1M a customer. For food or consumer products, it might be in the thousands of dollars. With these benchmarks, if the innovation team presents a plan to acquire a thousand, ten thousand, or even a hundred thousand customers over time, the investor or sponsor can get a good feel for the reasonableness of the total revenue projected for the business.

takes a lot of work to win a new customer, so why not design a revenue model that keeps getting more money from that customer? In this way, the repeat customer is a gift that keeps on giving. Investors look for recurring revenue in the financial planning of new ventures.

Define Price Level of Revenue Relative to Competitors

Price level relative to competitors is an important part of competitive positioning. The price level dimension within a revenue models generally falls into one of two categories:

1. A high price relative to current competitors. With this high price typically comes a *high margin*. High price, high margin ventures also tend to start off as low-volume business. Businesses that fit this description also tend to have selective retail distribution or direct selling to customers. These are expensive products and services and demand special selling methods.

2. A low price relative to competition. Low prices are also associated with *low- or moderate-margins*. Such businesses also tend to be higher volume in nature. Ventures with this profile try to make their money with volume.

For products, consider the automobile industry. Let's say that Honda sells about 500,000 Honda Accords in the United States each year, versus about 50,000 Acura MDXs, its popular high-end SUV. The margin on the Accord is smaller than the margin on an Acura, yet the volumes are ten times greater. These are two distinct revenue model approaches: moderate price, smaller margin, and high unit volume, versus premium price, higher margin, but lower volume on the other. Premium features are needed to support a premium price.

Services can also have the same price-differentiated revenue model. Consider a high-priced law firm. It may have perhaps 100 attorneys, some charging more than $600 per hour, and clients numbering in the low thousands. The legal work done by this type of law firm is customized for each client. Then consider Legal Zoom, a true services venture. It provides standardized legal services, low price but high volume, using software and the Web to automate document preparation. It will charge, for example, 10% to 20% of the price of a single hour with a face-to-face meeting with a premium attorney. Unlike a traditional law firm, Legal Zoom must draw tens of thousands of clients through its Web portal to generate its $200M plus in annual revenue.

As an entrepreneur, you must decide which type of business you wish to be— a high-price, relatively low-volume business, or a low-price, high-volume business. This decision will also drive your branding and the distribution channels and partners.

Sometimes, successful companies such as Apple, IBM, or EMC, (or companies that you don't often hear about, such as 3M), are able to get the best of both worlds: high prices relative to their competitors *together* with high volume. But this usually takes years of careful planning and operational excellence. The entrepreneur is best served by having a focus on one end of the spectrum or the other.

Our *own preference* for young entrepreneurs is to aim at better design, greater functionality, and higher prices relative to competitors. With this, you will be targeting customers who are looking for better solutions for their problems, and willing to pay a premium for those solutions. The reasons for our preference are multiple: (a) you can apply the "good, better, best" thinking to your offerings to

Figure 7.4
IBM's Business
Models

2014, Total Revenue ($000s): $92,793	Revenue In $000s	% of Total Revenue	Gross Profit
Global Technology Services (Outsourcing, integration)	37,130	40%	38%
Global Business Services (Consulting)	17,825	19%	31%
Software (Middleware and analytic tools	25,434	27%	89%
Systems and Technology (Large servers)	9,996	11%	40%
Global Financing	2,304	2%	48%

also reach mid-range buyers in your market segment; (b) you are more likely to realize operating profits on each dollar of sales, and do it earlier with your first customer sales; and (c) there are simply too many large and often offshore competitors already working the low-price, high-volume areas in nearly all industries.

Defining Distinct Streams of Revenue

Entrepreneurs often define multiple streams of revenue in their business models, the simplest examples being services in addition to products, or different types of services, or advertising plus subscription for Web businesses. Multiple streams of revenue are another form of leverage upon acquiring a single customer.

We can look at well-established examples. IBM's growth shows one of these. In the late 1990s and early 2000s, IBM had to transform itself from being primarily a computer hardware manufacturer with dwindling operating profit. In fact, IBM had about $40 billion in revenue at one point in the mid-1990s, yet managed to lose almost $8 billion in a single year! This near-death experience led to business model innovation in order to survive. The new strategy was to transform itself into a company that sells software and services as well as hardware. As shown in Figure 7.4, IBM actually developed five distinct streams of revenue: outsourcing services, consulting services, software, hardware, and financing. And each of these has a different profile in terms of operating profit. Software is incredibly profitable, while its consulting business is the least (because of the cost of labor for its business consultants).

How you form and count streams of revenue is important. If you are selling products, what other services might be sold as well. For example, a computer system needs ongoing maintenance and support. Or, a piece of industrial equipment might offer the opportunity to provide a range of accessories with it, even ones you do not create yourself but bring in from other third parties. Google relies 96% on advertising revenue from Adwords and related searched on Google searches. As a company, it is working hard to create different additional streams of revenue based on information products and services, as well as enterprise versions of Google Docs. Apple is perhaps the master at innovation that drives new streams of revenue: at last check, Apple derives 70% of its revenue from products and services (iPhone, iWatch) that did not exist five years ago.

Next, Define the Operating Model for Your Innovation

The components of the operating model are equally straightforward. We group these into four major buckets:

1. R&D
2. Production (Manufacturing, Fulfillment)
3. Go-to-Market (Distribution Channels, Marketing Partnerships)
4. Customer Service (Installation and Ongoing Support)

The operating model, i.e. the way the entrepreneur proposes to get things done in key parts of the business, is as important as revenue modeling for the innovator.

In general, innovation teams need to think lean when it comes to operations. This means working fast and effectively in all aspects of the business, and using partners wherever it makes sense and where there is little risk of losing or forfeiting your Intellectual Property.

The approach is not trying to *do everything yourself*. Focus on specific, value-added activities and partner with other companies, universities, or individuals for other activities. These third parties might help you get prototypes into the hands of customers more quickly, or be key partners in ongoing production or distribution.

For most innovators, the work you have done —gaining customer insight, creating the design of the product or service concept, developing the product/services strategy, and now, generating a powerful business model—all comprise your "value added" for the innovation. And you will keep doing it to adapt your innovation to changing market conditions. But to then proceed past the idea stage to actual implementation typically means first (a) developing prototyping of your products or services and quickly getting them into the hands of your target customers for feedback, then (b) actually producing those products and services in volume to generate revenue.

In each case—for the prototypes and the actual products or services to be provided to customers—you need to consider whether your own employees and equipment should be used to do the work, or to contract with other suppliers for that purpose. Contracting subcontracts is a form of **outsourcing** work. Doing what you do best and working with other partners to capture what they do best can be considered a lean approach to startup operations.

The reason why this is so important in the context of defining a business model is that it affects the upfront investment you need for people and machines, as well as ongoing operating expenses and margins based on whether your own staff performs a function, or others do it for you. Also, in-house versus outsourcing of R&D can easily affect your intellectual property position, which for technology ventures can be an important consideration for investors.

Defining Your Operating Model for R&D

Not all ventures need original research and development. A restaurant, a residential services business, or the typical consulting firm does not do R&D. But if your venture needs to create or integrate new technology, managing R&D is going to be important for success. Often, there is at least one strong technologist as a cofounder in a technology-intensive venture, be it a software, systems, or biotech company.

You would think that a technology-intensive venture would conduct all of its research and development in-house. However, increasingly R&D is partitioned into specific chunks of activity, some of which are done in-house by building an R&D staff, and others outsourced to third parties. This can affect not only the overall quality of the final product or service, but also the time to market and the amount of money needed to start and grow a company.

The question is, which aspects of R&D should be retained in the business and which can be outsourced?

To answer that question, ask yourself, "What are the things we want to do that will absolutely give us a competitive advantage and are essential in providing value to our customers?" Those activities are your "core competencies." Or better, let's call them your "secret sauce." In general, any part of the value-creating process that involves your "secret sauce"—whether it is R&D, production, or distribution—should be kept in-house.

If an activity does not involve a core competency, then carefully consider options for developing trusted external partners to whom you can outsource that work. Again, think "lean." Every single person in your company should be "high-value-added," contributing to some aspect of competitive advantage for your company. Of course, any time you outsource R&D, you need to develop an effective process for assessing the quality of what comes back. If you are starting a Web company and outsource the design and development of the Website to a third party, you still need to invest your time and that of key members of your team to review the work done by that outside firm. Your Website is the face of your company to the outside world!

For innovations creating complex systems with both hardware and software, it is not uncommon to see venture funds raised to pay for highly focused, external development of certain pieces of the overall system. The motivation for doing this is typically time to market. It takes at least six months to hire and integrate a first-rate software development team. The downside, of course, is that the crown jewels of the software company lie in a third-party developer, creating a dependency on that partner for ongoing improvements and bug fixes. It is more common these days to see a company keep its core software development in-house and, instead, farm out specific smaller developments, such as specialized reporting modules or hardware components to specialty R&D shops.

Outsourcing R&D is regularly done in the field of biotechnology. For example, drug discovery firms frequently contract with external research organizations to help "productize" new science. These outsourced activities include conducting analytical chemistry to identify and synthesize new compounds, setting up and conducting animal tests, and doing the same for human trials. Confidentiality and performance contracts are essential. By sharing important information with today's partner, the entrepreneur may be creating tomorrow's competitor.

A startup seldom has the cash to sue anyone. So hire outside help if you need it—but at first, give that outside contractor a small piece of the work. See if they perform and are reliable. Only then expand the relationship. Moreover, if you wish to create a business of lasting and substantial value, keep the "secret sauce"—the knowledge of customers' needs and wants and the design of your product or services—inside the company and in the hands of loyal employees.

Perhaps more fundamentally, even if you do not do formal "R&D," every firm needs to build and sustain insight into its customers, current and future. Customer insight is the most important core competency for any venture. *Never outsource the development of knowledge about your customers.*

Defining Your Operating Model for Production

For a complete business model, you also need to consider how to approach production and logistics. The use of third-party manufacturers has become commonplace. For startup ventures, this approach saves significant capital, avoiding the cost of purchasing, installing, operating, and servicing production equipment.

The drawback to outsourcing production is that a third-party contractor with access to the intellectual capital of the company, or its unique production process, may exploit it for its own benefit, legal agreements notwithstanding. This danger is particularly acute when companies use overseas contractors, who may be difficult to observe or control. On the other hand, experienced subcontract manufacturers tend to have a lot more manufacturing know-how than the entrepreneur, and can therefore be a valued partner. And the good subcontract manufacturers, in order to keep customers returning for more services, must be discrete in protecting their own customers' intellectual property.

Traditional product startups—food, beverage, and other consumer products—now regularly find contract manufacturers to produce finished goods and packaging. This is not always the case, however. Sometimes the manufacturing process is the secret sauce to the innovation, and it must be kept in-house. For example, one of our students started a new popcorn venture that uses sorghum instead of corn for its base material, produced gluten free for people suffering from Celiac disease. The entrepreneur bought a large industrial popcorn cooker from a company going out of business, and then modified it to pop sorghum. That entrepreneur's products were soon sold in Whole Foods stores across the United States. He used UPS for shipping.

Software does not involve much manufacturing, other than possibly printing documentation that is easily outsourced. However, a number of software startups are turning to Amazon and other "on demand" computer services vendors to rent computer time for software development—such as mathematical modeling—or compiling large software programs. As they see it, why buy computers that will be obsolete in a few years when they can capacity at low cost from Amazon? And when it comes time to put finished software into production for customers, most companies "host" their software on large servers run by third parties, with a level of security, systems backup, and scalability that few startups can afford.

Systems companies making some type of electronic device—such as specialized computing, industrial, or medical equipment—typically do the assembly of the first set of customer systems on their own for testing purposes. But after that, many startups are now turning to large third-party manufacturers such as Flextronics International. Here, too, the use of contractors for assembly and testing saves time and capital. The large contract manufacturers have achieved high levels of quality, low cost, and customer service. But you need to make sure that any contract manufacturer has a rock-solid reputation for timeliness of delivery and flexibility to make small configuration changes when a problem is found.

Services firms, by their nature, do nearly all "production" in-house. The service operation is the production plant. It is also the all-important "touch point" with customers, and as such is not a candidate for outsourcing. Financial services and information products ventures are also services organizations that do most information "manufacturing" or data mining in-house after aggregating data from both internal and external sources.

Defining Your Operating Model for Go-to-Market

In our experience, innovators consistently undervalue the importance of their "go-to- market" strategies and investment. By go-to-market, we refer to a company's plan to engage and deliver products and services to customers. Inexperienced innovators tend to focus instead on their technology and the products or services. This is wrong. The sales strategy must be just as powerful as the technology strategy. Products do not sell themselves.

A business's distribution channel is its pipeline to customers, and is often a key element in a successful business model. Staples, for example, innovated the first office supply "superstore." Dell famously bypassed the traditional retail channel, selling directly to PC buyers—first by phone and then online. When Apple opened the doors of its iTunes Music Store, it did so via the Internet. Now Apple's retail stores are so effective for its hardware and services that Best Buy—the leader in consumer electronics retailing—has seen its sales diminish in recent years.

There are a number of direct channels. The most obvious is a direct sales force —salespeople whom your company employs to sell its products, systems, or services to the customer. Innovations are well served having a good salesperson on the team from early on to help sell to the first one or two customers. Nothing proves the merit of an innovation like real customer money, and it typically takes great skill and persistence to achieve this for a company that is new and doesn't have any other customers! You also have to be very careful when bringing on salespeople. They need to have a track record of success in your target industry—with customers you can call to validate the salesperson's capabilities.

There are, of course, other direct channels. Your innovation might have its own retail stores or its own eCommerce Website. Or, you might find it best to propose a multichannel option in your business plan—combining a retail channel, for example, with a direct Web or mail order channel. For example, your authors sometimes purchase fishing gear from a company called Cabela's. It started off as a catalogue mail order business for outdoor sportsmen. It then opened its own retail stores, first in the Midwest, and has now expanded across the country. And it has a robust Web order business. Thus Cabela's has three channels, all of which are "direct to consumer." L. L. Bean does the same, as does Apple.

Then there are many different types of indirect channels or selling intermediaries. These include:

- **Retailers**, who obviously sell directly to the end-users or consumers of products. Increasingly, they are selling services as well. For example, in the pet food industry, PetSmart houses the Banfield veterinarian clinics, becoming a one-stop shop for the consumer. Your automotive dealer will try to sell you XM satellite radio and extended warranty services in addition to the vehicle itself. The business model implication is that retailers or dealers expect to make a 30% to 50% margin on the end-user price of a product, and generally, less margin for add-on services.

- **Distributors**, who are the intermediaries that perform a variety of distribution functions, including holding inventory and marketing to and supplying retailers. Typically, a distributor buys your products at a price that provides it with 5% to 10% margin on the final customer price of the product. That's the business model implication of using a distributor. Distributors tend to cover an entire region or country for a certain class of product or service. Wholesalers are typically synonymous with distributors.

- **Agents**, who are the intermediaries that market a product/service for a fee. These are often referred to as manufacturers' agents or selling agents. You might retain an agent, for example, to find distributors or retailers in a foreign market, or to get you into the front door of a large national retailer. Be sure to ask for evidence of the agent's effectiveness before signing an agreement! Many entrepreneurs have been promised "the moon," paid hefty monthly retainer fees for six months, and not seen a single penny in additional revenue. Don't be one of them!

- **Brokers**, who are the intermediaries that bring buyers and sellers together to negotiate purchases. They do not take title to anything, but tend to work on some type of commission basis, often 5% or so. You will find numerous brokers across the various financial services industries, for example.

- **OEMs**, who are the manufacturers through which you sell products or systems, where these are included as part of their manufactured products. An OEM contract with a large corporation offers the promise of high volumes for the entrepreneur, but also often results in a substantial discount (sometimes up to 70%) of the "list price" for a product. OEM partners like IBM, HP, or any other large company also take a lot of upfront work because your component or software has to be engineered to work in their own systems.

- **VARs,** who are the "value-added resellers" that buy your products (typically computer hardware and software or devices of some sort) and then add their own software and services as part of the sale to the customer. VARs tend also to expect a significant discount off your list price, in the range of 30% to 40%. The great thing about VARs in certain high-tech industries is that they are focused on a specific vertical market or niche and have highly specialized direct sales forces that work directly with accounts in that niche. At the same time, VARs need support. You will have to assign an engineer to work with the VAR's own engineering staff to learn how to make your products or systems function and integrate them with other technologies in their solution stack.

With indirect channels, you can also have a multichannel strategy—but here you must proceed with the utmost caution. Many software companies sell both through retailers and directly to consumers through the Web. Just think of Intuit or Symantec for examples of well-managed, multichannel strategies in software. Microsoft adds to this with a robust OEM strategy—with its software bundled by manufacturers onto their own computers.

However, having more than one channel raises the specter of *channel conflict*—offering two ways to buy the same product –that can confuse customers. It can lead various channel partners to begin to discount your products in order to get the sale. As soon as this happens, even the best product can be blemished. Salespeople tend to say the best things about the products with which they make the highest commissions. Moreover, a channel partner is making an important commitment to your company by carrying your product. This involves training its own sales force and co-marketing your product or service. They will be upset if your own sales force or Website steals customers. If you are going to use channel partners, your commitment must be to support *their sales* as best you can.

Becoming a channel for other companies that disintermediates current suppliers and channel members is a venture strategy in its own right. Disintermediation means the removal or bypassing of established channel players to reach customers directly. In many ways, the Web has disintermediated many industries, allowing producers of products and services to develop direct relationships with customers. Amazon disintermediates retailers. Or, Zappos is the powerful online fashion merchandiser specializing in contemporary shoes and apparel, backed up with best-in-class delivery and customer service. It disintermediated traditional shoe retailers. Started only in 1999 outside of Las Vegas as an online retailer, Zappos was approaching a billion dollars in sales before Amazon acquired it in 2010.

There is also a long- established history of successful software companies adding incremental streams of revenue by becoming channels for third-party software developers—part of the recurring revenue model we described above. The software company markets its ability to provide customers with access to other independent software firms. These firms build applications on top of the venture's own software, and are then marketed on the venture's Website as add-on applications. Not only does the venture receive a small sales commission, but it also presents a broader solutions portfolio to current and prospective customers. This is not disintermediation, per se, but it is becoming a channel in its own right— becoming a "Pied Piper" for a community of like-minded software developers.

As an entrepreneur, your go-to-market questions are:

- Where do my target customers prefer to buy the type of products or services I aim to sell?

- How much information do they require to make the purchase? If it is a lot—as in buying enterprise software—then you will need a direct sales force that can speak to the advantages of your products. And even if you use a direct sales force, the more information you can put on a self-service Website, the better.

- How important is convenience to these customers? If it is a major factor in their decisions, an eCommerce Website backed by UPS fulfillment might be the way to go.

- How do I build visibility and awareness for my products or services, and what are the realistic costs of achieving these ends, be they preferred placement or product sampling in a retailer, advertising in a magazine, search engine optimization, or even becoming a preferred merchant on Amazon? What are the best approaches for a strong launch into the market, and what are the financial implications of those approaches?

Defining Your Operating Model for Customer Service

Most innovators undervalue customer service before they start a company, but once the game is afoot, they appreciate the importance of promptly solving customers' problems.

There are obvious reasons. First, and most important, is that when you sell a product or service to customer, you have an obligation to that person or business to meet and fulfill the promise of your offering. This is a moral commitment that is one of those foundational elements that can make or break any business. It creates a reputation for honesty and integrity that stands by you as a person throughout your career. Customer service and support has deeper meaning beyond the individual transaction.

Second, strong customer service is the best way to insure that your current customers not only become recurring customers, but also, advocate for your company to other prospective customers. Customer service should not be considered just an operating expense, but rather, a way to build revenue. Do you want customers to say good things about your company? Sell them outstanding products and services – designed with the methods in the prior chapters and manufactured or otherwise produced with excellent quality –and then stand by your products to the very end, even if it costs you some money to take care of particularly problematic customer situations. Given the way that customers review and rate products and services on the Web, standing by your customers is not only a matter of honor, but also, good business.

Third, an operating model for providing service can also reveal new ways to make money. For example, your company might provide a basic level of service as part of the product purchase, but charge more for premium levels of service. One need only look at the "extra legroom" on economy (Delta Airlines calls this "Economy Comfort") as an example. Or access to on-board wireless services as another premium service. Apple provides another example of monetizing value-added services on top of a standard purchase. It provides AppleCare for about 15% of the purchase price of a new computer or mobile phone, a service that is not frequently used by most customers because Apple's products are so reliable. And Apple has even more services for additional money, such as One to One for personal computer training ($99 a year). For a senior person converting from a Windows machine, $100 a year is short money to receive high quality training in all the new software in a convenient location. Moreover, bringing customers back into the store provides them the opportunity to buy accessories. Apple also has AppleCare for Enterprise, complementing its new partnership with IBM to bring a new class of industry specific mobile solutions based on iOS. Apple views customer service as a revenue generating and brand building activity.

An operating model for customer service can be constructed by developing a workflow of the customer service process or transaction. As you do this, consider the following:

- **Warranties:** is there is a standard warranty with the product, as part of the purchase, and for what period of time?

- **Return services:** is there a special service for customer returns? For example, most fishing fly rod manufacturers provide a 25-year warranty on their products but with a $25 fee for any and all returns during that time period. $25 is nothing for the fisherman who has paid $800 for his or her new toy and who has a 25 year assurance of repair upon breakage. Many different types of businesses have a return and repair shipping service arranged with UPS, for example.

- **Tiers of support:** For IT-related companies, there are often levels of support designed into the total support system. Tier 1 can be considered the front line (with its own dedicated toll-free number) where all calls are received and most problems handled. Problems without quick resolution are escalated to a more specialized team of technical experts. Every interaction should be tracked in a software system (For example, look at desk.com for $30 per month.) The tiered approach also works well if you are selling through certain intermediaries, who you train to cover the first line of support and provide a highly responsive pathway for problems they cannot solve.

- **Customer support staff:** In most startups, founders and employees double-up as customer support staff. Depending on the type of business, this can be viable solution for an extended period of time. However, once your customer population grows to a certain level, it makes sense to allocate dedicated resources to the task. The reason is that you do not want your most expensive, most valuable employees taking too many customer service telephone calls. For example, in a software company, you want your best developers programming new code, not assisting customers with basic software guidance or bug reporting.

- **Outsourcing customer support:** Outsourcing customer support is method to reduce operating expense and relieve stress for a rapidly growing business – but it obviously entails substantial risk. It is growing industry. The entrepreneur can find suppliers who will handle customer support through email, call centers, and social media monitoring companies. If you decide to investigate this option, look for outsources that have clients you can call for references. Call centers need to provide an incentive system for their own employees as well. Alternatively, if you have the type of business where your needs for customer service are minimal in the beginning, you can also locate individual subcontractors hired on a part-time basis, who you train in providing support for your product, and who work out of their home offices. A 1-800 telephone number (or the equivalent toll free number in your country) can be directed to these subcontractors. Here, too, having subcontractors use your company's software for tracking customer support is essential.

As a venture grows, customer service tends to be brought back inside the company to insure quality – and to provide opportunities for upselling current customers new products and services.

Some Final Words of Caution on Popular Business Model Trends

Please, don't give value away for free! *You might provide users with the ability to test a product or service at no cost for a little while, but soon the meter needs to start running.*

Innovators often make the mistake of creating a next-generation product, system, or service that is a lot better than anything currently in the marketplace, and then charge less for it than those competitors offering inferior products. They think that this is the best way to ramp up sales. The problem is that a great product, system, or service is nothing if it does not also lead to a financially successful company. At some point, sooner, rather than later, your innovation will have to start generating cash from operations. If you train customers to get a lot and not pay a lot, it will be very difficult to get them to switch into a pay-more mode. It is also very difficult to support a flood of new customers in any new venture. We believe it is better to get a solid, yet constrained, initial set of customers and serve them well. Learn what it takes to be a successful enterprise. Then raise the capital required to scale the business.

Consider EMC, started by the late Dick Egan and his partner, Roger Marino[1]. They started selling office furniture to generate cash to fund R&D for the product they really wanted to sell: a large-scale storage system to take on existing systems from IBM. EMC deployed a new architecture—called RAID—that permitted customers to hot-swap added storage arrays to their system. This allowed their systems to be more powerful yet have a lower cost of goods by using more common PC disks than other high-end systems on the market (which used rarer 15-inch disks). Egan

---

1 Both Dick Egan and Roger Marino were alums of our university, Northeastern University. They were famous for hiring smart Israeli and Irish engineers, while recruiting collegiate varsity athletes from local colleges as salespeople. The third key player in EMC was Moshe Yanai, the longtime head of R&D. Moshe served in the Israeli defense forces and brought intelligence, determination, and discipline to engineering. He would sometimes fly a helicopter to staff meetings held at Northeastern's off-campus conference center.

and Marino could have charged less than IBM, since their cost of goods was less. Instead, they priced their products at a 25% premium over IBM because EMC's RAID systems were 25% faster and more scalable. EMC grew to become the market leader in enterprise storage with over $20 billion in annual revenue, and only in 2016, became part of Dell. For decades, EMC worked hard to understand, deliver, and price to customer value.

Our advice to you: Try to resist the allure of gaining mass numbers by giving products and services away completely for free. This relegates making operating profits from each new customer unlikely for a number of years. Sooner or later, the chickens will come home to roost. Your investors will want to see cash generated from each sale. In fact, a worthy goal is that a business model should seek profitability on the very first sale. Even if you have difficulty achieving this right away, it will provide the mindset and discipline needed for long-term success. It doesn't necessarily have to be cheaper—just better.

Of course, Facebook may end up being the great counter-example. We know that Facebook sounds attractive to young innovators—a founder who started developing the concept in college, gives his primary services away for free to get the "eyeballs" needed to support an advertising revenue model, and becomes a billionaire in the process! But now, Facebook is leveraging its eyeballs to generate close to $15 billion in annual revenue from advertising, with nearly a 65% gross profit, all fueled by the growth of mobile data.

READER EXERCISES

Let's create a business model for your innovation. Figure 7.5 presents the basic questions you need to ask and answer for each part of a business model.

Think back to the innovation focus and product/services strategy you developed in previous chapters. You should have (a) your target industry segment/niche, (b) the target customer(s) within that niche and their primary uses that you will be improving, (c) your products and/or services offerings, and (d) the positioning of those offerings relative to competitors. This is a great foundation from which to develop a business model.

Step 1: Define the Revenue Model

Begin at the top row—the revenue model. Write in a phrase or two to describe the four dimensions of your revenue model. If you are selling both products and services, you will need to specify the type, frequency, and price level relative to competition for each, respectively. More generally, how many streams of revenue are you shooting for? Will there be recurring revenue? (We hope so!) Can you achieve premium pricing?

As you answer these questions, think beyond the startup phase to a scaled-up version of your business three to five years down the road. Map this out on a whiteboard, and then fill in the worksheet. For your choices, state your rationale for anything that doesn't seem

Figure 7.5
Business Model Questions

Revenue Model	• Type of revenue? (licensing, subscription, freemium, free w/advertising, retail) • Price: relative to competition (Hi, Med, Low) • Volume: Amount of product/service in a purchase • Velocity: Is there more than one product or stream of revenue in a purchase? • Frequency: Is it recurring? Once a day/month/year/forever?
Operating Model Needed to Produce the Revenue	
For R&D	• How long will it take to develop your first product? - Time to alpha, beta, commercial release? • In-house – outsource? Cost of each in terms of labor. Time for each. • Is there IP? How does this R&D approach fit with the IP strategy?
For Production	• How will product be manufactured? In-house, outsourced? • What is the cost (OpEx, Capex) of the option selected? • What is the per-unit cost target? • What is the time to implement the option you choose? • What is the initial order required to launch to market?
For Go-to-market	• What is the channel to get to the product or service to the customer? Is there a secondary channel? • Draw out the entire sales funnel. How do the #'s of customers transform at each stage of the funnel? • What margin does the channel consume on the retail price of the product or service? • What investment does it take to build the channel – for the first year, and the next several years?
For Installation & Service	• Is there a shipping charge? How much is it? • Does your product or service need on-site installation or integration? Who does it? Is the cost of this included in the sale price, and if so how much? How long does installation/integration take? • If you are charging for installation / customization / service, what is that revenue and cost model?

obvious. Are there analogies in the market that help show that your revenue model is feasible and scalable? How is it the same, or different, than current players who operate in your chosen market niche?

After drawing your product line/services strategy, make a set of bullet points that contains the common features of your product or services portfolio. These might be a certain type of styling or packaging, a certain type of engine or microprocessor, a common user interface, or certain service guarantees. Later on, once you are building your company, these will turn into common platforms for your products or services—things that you can leverage across the entire portfolio.

Now step back. Take a look at the result with your team members. Does the combination of products and services set the foundation for an exciting, growing business? How can you make it even more exciting?

Step 2: Define the Models for R&D, Production, and Go-to-Market

Do the same for your approach to R&D, manufacturing or production (fulfillment for services), and branding and distribution. Once again, always ask yourself why your approach for each area makes sense and if there are analogies in the marketplace. What is the reasoning behind these decisions? Also, we want you to anticipate the learning in Section II of this book by already thinking about the financial implications for the amount of startup capital needed to start your company and get to the moment of actual product or service launch. Be smart about this. If there are suppliers or channel partners with good reputations in your market niche, consider working with them. In the beginning of any venture, your goal should be to minimize fixed costs (lease office space, do not buy the building!), and instead, make them variable expenses. The less you have to raise, the less stock you have to give up as a founding team. Then, of course, the goal is to provide enough value in your products or services so you can charge a sufficient price to generate the operating profit needed to grow the business—and, potentially, bring some of these external activities back into the business as part of a scaled-up business model.

Step 3: Integrate

Take a step back. Consider your models for revenue, R&D, production, and go-to-market. How well do the four rows in Figure 7.6 integrate for your innovation integrate? Do they make for a single powerful, cohesive whole? If not, re-examine your reasoning for the dimensions that seem to be out of fit. You need to get this right!

At this point, we encourage you to organize a show-and-tell session for your business model with your professor and your classmates. Show your product or service concept, your proposed portfolio, and your business model as a package. This is the time to use your business model to bring the complete venture concept together.

As with all prior chapters, it might be time to pivot on your venture idea, or, in a less dramatic way, refine your Customer Value Proposition. If you cannot find a good business model to power your new product or service, a pivot may be necessary. But keep working the idea first before giving up. In terms of refining, thinking about how you charge for things can add to or improve your Customer Value Proposition, e.g. by deferring a large, up-front purchase price through a subscription model, or by providing professional services on top of a high-tech or IT-centric product.

Figure 7.6
Define and Integrate
the Business Model
for an Innovation

Business Model Dimensions	The Approach for Your Venture	Rationale for that Approach
REVENUE MODEL Types of revenue Frequency of revenue Price level relative to competitors Multiple streams of revenue		
Operating model for R&D Build technology or buy ? What is the "focus" of internal versus external R&D?		
Operating model for Production Manufacturing – internal or outsourced ? Logistics – internal or outsourced?		
Operating model for Go to Market Channel ? Marketing partners?		
Operating model for Customer Service Through channel partners? Direct? Tiers of customer service? Warrantees, free, charge?		
	TAKEN AS A WHOLE, DO THESE ALL FIT TOGETHER? How does this business model compare to other firms Competing in your target market?	

A business model can be as innovative and important as any product or service itself. Think hard about yours because it lies at the core of any truly successful venture. And a business model will have profound implications for the resources requested for implementation – such as whether to buy a machine or outsource manufacturing, or to build a large salesforce or sell through partners. The business model will drive the financial projections that we will learn how to prepare in the second half of this book.

TESTING AN INNOVATION:
Conduct a Reality Check !

8

The Purpose of the Chapter

Every year, millions of innovators come up with ideas that they believe could be the beginning of a great startup or new product or service inside an existing company or public sector organizations. While many of these concepts may seem to be outstanding from a 50,000-foot level, talk is cheap. Any innovator worth his or her salt must test how attractive the innovation concept is perceived with target customers. One way to do this is do develop prototypes of an MVP and show them to customers. Another way is to do a more formal survey. We want you to do both. *Each provides important information*.

Now it is time to put your work to a last, powerful test. In this chapter, we are going to do a field-based Reality Check for an innovation idea. It is a structured survey with some specific analysis. It is a fast, effective, and gives you additional ammunition with which to convince yourself and others that your idea is indeed customer-driven.

Please note that this type of Reality Check is a complement to the prototyping and customer validation we learned before, e.g. developing an MVP and showing it to customers. All innovators should build a prototype of their new product or service idea, show it to customers, learn, improve, and show it to them once again, and learn some more. A survey merely adds additional empirical proof for the prototyping process.

For this Reality Check, it is time to go back into the field to talk to customers, but this time, in greater numbers and armed with a more formal survey instrument. Your goal remains to become more expert about your target customers and their core needs than anyone else—*including your professors*!

Learning Objectives

- Plan the "Reality Check."
- Define specific questions to test your Customer Value Proposition, as well questions to test your product or service solutions, the revenue dimensions of your business model, and your go-to-market strategy.
- Organize customer panels—the interviewees—with an eye toward getting this research done in one or two weeks.
- Conduct the field research itself—methods that work best for approaching end-users and buyers whom you don't already know.
- Analyze the results of the field research.

The First Step:
A Final Edit of the Customer Value Proposition

In preparing your Customer Value Proposition to show to customers as part of a survey, you need it to be incredibly clear, crisp, and focused on benefits and competitive differentiation.

A refined Customer Value Proposition is something you can either say to customers or have them read in less than 30 seconds, have them understand it, and be ready to answer some questions about it.

As we have learned, the Customer Value Proposition has a specific structure with the following components:

* The brand name (of the group of products/services)

* The specific problem solved

* The specific target customer and specific use case

* The specific target buyers (this can be optional in the survey if it gets too complicated to explain to the respondent)

* Specific benefits for customers (in terms of features, performance, quality, and/or price/revenue model)

* Competitive differentiation from current products/services and what is the basis for customer preference when buying

You just improved your Customer Value Proposition with positioning and branding information in the prior chapter. This is one last shot at revision for the customer survey. Now, if we put all of the items together in a textual format:

> ABC is a new family of products (or services) that [solves what problem] for [which target customers] in [which specific use cases]. The benefits that we expect to provide include [name the major specific benefits]. ABC will stand out from all competitors because of because of its [positioning on functional, emotional, and social dimensions] for customers.

The format does not have to follow precisely the structure above, but make sure your Customer Value Proposition contains the information. We will be using the pet snack venture as an example for the rest of this chapter, so let's look at the Customer Value Proposition refined for the Reality Check:

> HealthyWags is a special treat made for dog owners who truly love their pets. It is healthy, nutritious, and tastes great, made by a company that is local and people you can trust. Unlike the large mass manufacturers that use animal by-products from foreign suppliers, and produce their snacks in huge plants, we source all of our ingredients locally and bake them fresh in small ovens right in Boston. We use all-natural ingredients and have the

meaty flavors that dogs relish. We will also carry nonmeat snacks for those of you who prefer only grains and vegetables. We use 100% recycled materials in our artisanal, heritage style packaging. Our snacks will keep your pet healthy and provide a snack they truly relish. It is a clear, simple way to show your care and love for your pet.

Now take a moment to write down any changes. Make the paragraph as clear and powerful as possible. It really makes a difference for this type of survey work. Prototypes or sketches will make the Customer Value Proposition all the more real.

The Questions Following the Customer Value Proposition

The next step is to develop specific questions that test different aspects of your Customer Value Proposition, the product or service design, and the business model. The questions will also help you forecast the potential revenue for your innovation.

Look at Figure 8.1. This figure contains questions to ask customers. You should provide your Customer Value Proposition on a separate page, which will be handed out to participants so they can refer back to it as you work through the questions.

The questions shown in Figure 8.1 help customers assess the attractiveness of the Customer Value Proposition, as well as important aspects of the business model. It also tests the degree to which customers like the solutions they already have now – hence the term Reality Check. The questions will also test your competitive positioning and distinctiveness, and give a measure of the all important purchase intent, as well as the frequency and amount of purchase. We also want you to get information about the customer's preferred point of purchase, be it a store, the Web, or face to face, and the preferred venues for learning about offerings such as yours. This holds for a product, a Mobile app, or a more traditional service. Lastly, the questions in the Reality Check can be used to find complementary products and services that customers might want in addition to those proposed in your Customer Value Proposition. These complementary products or services can help you think about partnerships with other companies, or R&D opportunities for the future.

Now take a few minutes to work down the questions in Figure 8.1, but with pencil in hand. Jot down some notes on how you might modify these questions, if at all, for your own survey. You can also add one or two additional questions – be fore-warned, usually ten questions is the limit for customers, especially after the first two setup questions in Figure 8.1 that are more general in nature. We would not recommend eliminating any of the questions currently in Figure 8.1.

Organizing Customer Panels

Many of you by now have one primary target customer group, and based on your fieldwork, feel confident that you are on track. But we have worked with enough teams over the years to know that some might still be debating the best market target market segment for their ideas. This Reality Check is the perfect opportunity to determine the correct focus.

Figure 8.1
The Field Research
Instrument for the
Reality Check

The Field Research Instrument for the Reality Check

(To be applied with different potential target customers. Provide your Venture Concept Statement for Customers on a separate page. Also, provide a simple description of your product or service, using a sketch or diagram if this helps customers understand your venture.)

First, can you tell us a little bit about yourself or your company? (Open-ended, but look for key demographic descriptors to align with your market segmentation and customer groups.)

This is what our product or service generally does (Provide a quick description or a picture/sketch on a separate page.) Do you view yourself as a potential customer of this offering? (If yes, continue.) What would be the different ways that you would want to use the product or service?

1. How satisfied are you with the current products/services you use now?

Very dissatisfied   Dissatisfied   Neither Dis/Sat.   Satisfied   Very Satisfied

2. Do you see the proposed offering as distinctive from the competitors?

Not different   Somewhat different   Highly distinctive

3. How much would you be willing to pay for this offering for this offering compared to the current products/services you use now?

Less   Same   More

4. How often do you buy similar products or services? (Open-ended.)

5. How much do you spend each time you make a purchase? (Open-ended, but looking for a dollar amount.) Do you prefer to buy, rent, subscribe, etc? (Try to validate the structure of revenue.)

6. Where is the best place to buy products/services such as this? (Open-ended, but look for a specific preferred channel and ways in which they test or try products/services.)

7. Where do you get your information about products/services such as this? (Open-ended. Look for preferred information sources.)

8. How likely is it that you would be willing to buy this offering?

Very unlikely   Unlikely   Neither   Likely   Very Likely

9. What additional features do you think are important in a product or service such as this? (Open-ended)

For example, a team of graduate students created a new modular jewelry concept that allowed women to personally customize their jewelry for day, evening, work, or social occasions, with color variations matching the clothes being worn. As students themselves, they initially targeted young women still in school. But in their ethnography and Reality Check, they also talked to young professional women recently out of school. The concept was tested against both customer groups. As one might expect, it was the somewhat older professional women who wanted modular, flexible fashion items even more. The Reality Check made this customer focus clear. Too often, student teams think that they themselves are the only or the best target user. And just as often, that is not the case!

Therefore, we want you to structure customers into distinct groups (following your segmentation work an early chapter) and then ask representative members of each group for their thoughts on your innovation idea. It might take a little more work to do multiple customer groups, but the benefits can be tremendous. In this way, you can use the Reality Check to make sure you have targeted the best customer group for your products or services, and that your offerings are positioned appropriately for their tastes and preferences. It will also help you appreciate how the different groups vary. And you might actually find a better set of customers for launching your innovation (such as those who have more money to spend or have greater need of your solutions). Or you might learn what needs to be added to your product line or services to expand your business for the next stage of growth.

Whereas before, we encouraged you to spend time with and interview six to 12 customers for each stage of the learning; here we want you to aim for thirty or more respondents per customer group for the survey. Many teams walk in with survey samples of fifty or more customers – and these always tend to have the strongest findings, either positive or negative. On the other hand, if your project is a B2B innovation, you will do well to talk to managers in twenty companies, or even a dozen companies. Access to enterprise customers tends to be far more challenging than for consumer products or services.

Conducting the Field Research

We need an example to show you how a survey is designed, administered, and then analyzed. Since your authors love their pets, and we assume many of you grew up in households with your favorite dog or cat, we are going to use the pet snack example form earlier chapters to continue forward. The example -- HealthyWags – is based on a real venture. Let's do the Reality Check that they did for premium snacks for dogs.

As a quick exercise for organizing customer panels for this Reality Check, pretend that you are a dog owner and are answering a respondent answering the questions for a pet snack innovation team at a dog park near your school. Pretend (or not!) that you are a young professional woman, single or married, and have a dog (Spot) with which you have a special, almost mother-child relationship. You tend to shop at Whole Foods grocery store for food generally, buy all-natural pet food brands sold there, and spend whatever time it takes at your veterinarian to keep Spot healthy. You are skeptical of mass-manufactured, non-local products made with mystery ingredients. When it comes to snacks for both yourself and your dog, you explicitly read labels and look for natural, healthy ingredients. In fact, you want something for you dog that feels like the types of snacks you would want for yourself. For some of you, these might be vegetable only proteins instead of meat. And over the past several years, increasingly you have been shopping at a pet specialty store such as PetSmart of Petco to see a much broader variety of premium pet foods and snacks, made by smaller, independent manufacturers, some of them local to your region.

Next, switch your customer group by virtue of demographics, attitudes, and behaviors. Let's be Mom with two kids who buys pet food and snacks while she is shopping at the local grocery store for the rest of her family. She seeks a combination of good quality and reasonable price, and for this, prefer well-established pet food brands such as Purina, Pedigree, or Iams. For her, the pet is another member of the family and when it comes to food, treated at a level below that of her children, but above her husband!

Last, let's pretend to be a dog owner who has a more distant relationship with your pet. Say you live in the countryside, are a 60 year-old male, and view your dog not only as a companion but also as a guard dog. You shop at Walmart for inexpensive pet food in bulk. You have rarely been to the vet. You also make the animal sleep in the mudroom. And you feed your pet cheap cookies for snacks.

In each role, if you were to answer a Reality Check survey, the answers would come out very differently, boiling down preferences to quality, price, brand, and channel. *As an innovator, this is exactly the type of information you need to know for targeting and execution.*

We have seen the same approach work just as well for B2B innovations. A biomedical device team might have a series of potential applications for a new diagnostic technology coming out of the research lab—but it is only when team members talk to actual doctors that they find the one or two compelling applications on which physicians will actually spend time and money.

We think that it is important to challenge yourself to get feedback from members of adjacent customer groups. You might find, in fact, that your original idea appeals more strongly to a group of customers different from your original target. Or, you might also find ways to expand or refine your core offering to adjacent customers in the target market. Beyond simple validation, the Reality Check is all about refining your targeting and fleshing out your product or services strategy with a more empirical method. And even while you are administering your survey, you can also ask follow-on questions. *Listening* to customers is the best way *to learn.*

Let's Explore the Survey Methods with an Example

In earlier chapters, we had you observe and talk to target customers to gain the insights into the user needs needed to drive the design of your solutions. Now we are seeking more specific responses—data—for more specific things. You will be generating these data by asking people questions and recording their responses. You have several options for doing this. You can collect the data by:

- Personal interviews (face to face) following a structured discussion guide

- Telephone interviews also following a structured discussion guide

- Mailed surveys that respondents complete and mail back to you

- Online surveys, using one of the popular survey tools offered on the Web. You can find a number of such tools that you can use at no initial cost with a simple Google search.

Personal interviews (face to face) have the major advantage of enabling you to ask probing questions or see reactions of the respondents. But personal interviews can be time consuming and expensive to conduct, particularly if the people you want to talk to live in a different city or region. Yet, just as we learned before, any face-to-face time with a target customer is worth its weight in gold to the innovator. You simply cannot get enough of it—and this is our preferred method for testing Customer Value Propositions, product strategies, revenue models, and go-to-market approaches. As we also learned, try to do this research in situ—in the customer's actual buying and usage environment. Do your survey work in an environment that is most comfortable for the respondent, e.g. in their home turf, not yours.

As for the other possible methods, collecting data by mail can be slow and response rates low. Also, in mailed surveys, there may be bias in the data because those likely to respond will typically have either strong positive or negative reactions to your idea. Additionally, a mailed survey does not give you the flexibility to explain to the customer what you mean by a particular question. Often, customers misunderstand what you mean or simply get lost and therefore fail to complete a research instrument. Mail seems to be something of the past.

Collecting data by telephone allows the flexibility to talk to customers and walk through a research instrument. For business-to-business (B2B) innovations, we have seen this method used to great effect, grabbing 15 minutes of a busy manager's time to run through a set of important questions. However, for business-to-consumer (B2C) innovations, the telephone method is becoming increasingly difficult because consumers are sick and tired of marketing calls. Also, with many unlisted telephone numbers, it is becoming harder and harder to obtain a good sample of respondents.

Using the Web to collect data, on the other hand, is becoming increasingly popular. In our classes, we find that student teams have no trouble finding a 100 people or more to complete their online "concept tests." On the other hand, it's hard to get insight from the follow-on questions to the survey. Most often, the best insights come from such conversations.

Importantly, another key driver you must consider when determining a data collection method is whether or not you wish to present a "prototype," or visual of your core offering. If you have a good sketch of your new product idea, this can be included right beneath the Customer Value Proposition. Visuals always bring a concept to life for target customers. We strongly encourage you to use pictures and sketches whenever possible.

If it is important for the potential customer to actually see the prototype, then this stage of the research needs to be either face to face, or through conferencing software such as Skype. Never underestimate the power of Skype! Many of our students have used it to interview customers who live in different geographies or even different countries. Seeing the other person makes a difference and establishes trust far better than just a telephone call. And, you can demonstrate a prototype to reasonable extent on Skype.

Analyzing Your Data and Interpreting the Results

So let's say that you have designed your key questions, identified target customers and buyers, and have reached them either face to face, through the phone, or through the Web. You have gathered data for these questions and are ready to start your analysis. The purpose now is to consolidate what you have learned about the demographics, attitudes, behaviors, and core needs of the potential target customer groups you have identified, and then to validate your product/services strategy and its competitive positioning.

You must first consolidate all the data from the survey into a simple, single source of information. We will use the HealthyWags case as an illustration of a consolidated data set for a Reality Check.

Validating the Core Needs, Attitudes, Behaviors, and Demographics of Your Target Market

Successful innovators become experts in their target customers and their uses for a product or service. Take a quick look at what might emerge from a Reality Check

Figure 8.2
HealthyWags Consolidated Field Research Data: Questions 1 and 2

Opening General Question. Can you tell us a little bit about yourself or your company? (Open-ended, but look for key demographic descriptors to align with your market segmentation and customer groups.)

Results: (Combination of earlier ethnography and the Reality Check field research.)

Mother Goose (Attitude: Dog as family member, but still a pet.) Customers are health conscious when purchasing at the grocery store, and many are going to Whole Foods. They expect quality ingredients, but they are not label readers. They are explicitly focused on taste but value is also important because dog snacks are part of the overall household food budget. They will accept fortification of ingredients, as opposed to all-natural recipes. Tend to trust large brand name manufacturers. Shop in grocery stores or Target. Key motivation for feeding snacks: "I feed my dogs just for love." Key target customer. Estimated 50% of market based on industry reports. N=30.

Dog Mommy (Attitude: Dog as family member, dog as child – and may be a surrogate child for some.) Customers are very health conscious. These customers want quality ingredients and not at lot of fat and calories. All-natural is another key driver. Distrust large manufacturers. Want locally sourced food. They want all-natural ingredients, good taste, and minimally processed products. They are deliberate shoppers that read the ingredient list. Shop in Wholefoods, Trader Joes, and for pets, PetSmart, Petco, or independent pet retailers. Key motivation for feeding snacks: "I want my dog to be as healthy as I am." Key target customer. Estimated 30% of market based on industry reports. N=30.

Pet Buddy (Attitude: Dog as pet friend.) Predominantly male. They are focused on ingredients on a more scientific basis. All-natural is less of a concern. He does not mind using a dog snack as an indulgence. Milk Bones will do for this customer. Key motivation for feeding snacks: "If he is happy, I am happy." Looks at dog as exercise buddy. Estimated 20% of market based on industry reports. N=30.

Customer Value Proposition: This is our product or service, what it does, its' benefits, and how we think it is different than current competitors:

Supplement the Customer Value Proposition with pictures, sketches and prototypes.

for HealthyWags. Our focus here is primarily on Questions 1 and 2 of the Field Research Discussion Guide.

Opener. Can you tell us a little bit about yourself or your company? [Open-ended, but look for key demographic descriptors to align with your market segmentation and customer groups.]

Customer Value Proposition, Pictures, Sketches, Prototypes. This is what our product or service generally does [provide a quick description or a picture/sketch on a separate page].

Figure 8.2 shows a set of consolidated findings for the first opening general question in the Reality Check. The sample for this particular Reality Check is 90 dog owners, gathered by speaking with people in their neighborhoods or dog-walking parks. Three distinct customer groups emerged from this research as distinguished by owners' attitudes and behaviors toward pets, called by their persona names: Mother Goose (Mom with kids), Dog Mommy (professional woman, no kids), and Pet Buddy (Boomer Men). Demographics supported this customer grouping. Figure 8.3A provides specific descriptions for each. Those descriptions contain useful information on attitudes and behaviors, both of which drive products and service designs.

These are the types of insights we want you to have for your various potential target customer groups. Figure 8.2 contains further information about each customer group. Not every target customer will fit perfectly into one of your specific groups, but there should be strong alignment by virtue of shared needs, attitudes, behaviors, and perhaps demographics.

Validating Your Product or Services Design

The next step is to validate the attractiveness of your product or service idea of your innovation with the target customers. There are several aspects to this: (a) the extent to which the customers are dissatisfied with their current solutions, (b) the extent to which they find your solution distinctive (special and meaningful for their use case application), and (c) their purchase intent. You also want to know what additional product or service functionality they would like to see in your innovation.

The stars align for your innovation if target customers are highly dissatisfied with current solutions; your offerings are perceived as special, and show high purchase intent. Also, customers might be very interested in your idea conceptually, but if they are already pleased with their current product or service, it will be hard to get a high percentage to switch. Or they might perceive your concept as special but not special enough to support healthy pricing.

Turning to the HealthyWags' consolidated data (Figure 8.3), it is clear that certain target customers appreciate the premium, all-natural, healthy positioning. The Reality Check showed that premium features—all-natural nutrition—would command a price premium over current snacks. Let's take a look at the actual data:

Figure 8.3
HealthyWags
Consolidated Data:
Product/ Service
Design Questions

Question 1: How satisfied are you with the current products/services you use now?

Very dissatisfied   *Dissatisfied*   *Neither Dis/Sat.*   *Satisfied Very Satisfied*

      Mother Goose: 30% Dissatisfied or Very Dissatisfied
      Dog Mommy: 40% Dissatisfied or Very Dissatisfied
      Pet Buddy: 5% Dissatisfied or Very Dissatisfied

Question 2: Do you see the proposed offering as distinctive from the competitors?

Not different   *Somewhat different*   *Highly distinctive*

      Mother Goose: 20% Highly Distinctive
      Dog Mommy: 30% Highly Distinctive
      Pet Buddy: 10% Highly Distinctive

Question 8: How likely is it that you would be willing to buy this offering?

Very unlikely   *Unlikely Neither*   *Likely*   *Very Likely*

      Mother Goose: 25% likely/very likely
      Dog Mommy: 50% likely/very likely
      Pet Buddy: 10% likely/very likely

Question 9: What additional features would make you more likely to buy this (product or service)? (Open-ended.)

      Mother Goose: Bulk packaging to buy it for less money per lb.
                                Want smaller portion treats for training purposes.
      Dog Mommy: A no-meat version because "I don't eat meat myself."
      Pet Buddy :   "Can you make it look like a bone?"

Question 1: How satisfied are you with the current products/services you use now?

Very dissatisfied   Dissatisfied   Neither Dis. nor   Satisfied   Very satisfied
Satisfied

Mother Goose	20% Dissatisfied or Very dissatisfied
Dog Mommy	40% Dissatisfied or Very dissatisfied
Pet Buddy	5% Dissatisfied or Very dissatisfied

Those "Dog Mommy" customers—younger females who view their pet as their child—show the highest level of dissatisfaction with current pet snacks. This makes them a primary target customer for the innovation. That's what you need to find for your innovation. Conversely, those "Pet Buddy" males did not to really care about the quality of snacks (including for themselves!). Those are the type of customers that you need to know about ahead of time so that you don't waste your product development, distribution, and marketing money on them.

Question 2: Do you see the proposed offering as distinctive from the competitors?

Not different   Somewhat different   Highly distinctive

Mother Goose	20% Highly distinctive
Dog Mommy	30% Highly distinctive
Pet Buddy	10% Highly distinctive

Question 8: How likely is it that you would be willing to buy this offering?

Very unlikely   Unlikely   Neither likely   Likely   Very likely
*   or unlikely*

Mother Goose	25% Likely/Very likely
Dog Mommy	50% Likely/Very likely
Pet Buddy	10% Likely/Very likely

The Customer Value Proposition for HealthyWags aligns best with the younger female, e.g. Dog Mommy, as shown with the purchase intent Question 8. She has the highest level of appreciation for the proposed product and will support it with her spending. Mother Goose comes in a strong second; Pet Buddy's a distant third.

The Reality Check can also provide support for having a variety of "good, better, best" components within a product line, as well as complementary products or services. This is the purpose of the very last, open-ended question in the Field Research Discussion Guide, and it is presented as a way to increase the customers' perception of his or her likelihood of purchase if they would like to see additional features or offerings.

Question 9: What additional features would make you more likely to buy this [product or service]? [Open ended]

For example, a Mother Goose response to Question 9 was to ask for bulk packaging to buy it for less money per pound; smaller-portioned treats for training purposes. These grocery shoppers are always thinking about the family budget; therefore, bulk packaging would make sense. Also, being experienced in training (children as well as pets), it makes sense that these customers might want a new type of healthier training snack in a "bite-size" portion.

For the Dog Mommy, one of the responses to Question 9 was: "A no-meat version because "I don't eat meat myself." The Dog Mommy customer—that younger female typically not yet with children and who views her pet as her child—is very much focused on her own eating needs when she thinks about the pet. Eating less meat is a growing trend among such consumers, and therefore that preference is passed onto the pet (even though dogs clearly love to eat meat!).

For Pet Buddy, a really interesting Question 9 response was "Can you make it look like a bone?" This male dog owner is thinking about play and enjoyment with his pet: "Since dogs love bones, why not make it look like a bone?" Any of these ideas might be introduced at startup or later on once the business picks up steam.

Validating Your Go-to-Market Strategy

Testing your commercialization approach in terms of channel and pricing as important for innovators as the product or service design. Innovators often focus so hard on their products or services that they short-change the go-to-market aspects of the business. Go-to-market is the hidden genie of any successful new product or service development. A bad salesperson or low-quality retailer can make the best products appear inferior. Or conversely, as we have seen so often in Web innovations, developing communities around a new product or service can create the buzz needed to generate critical momentum in a marketplace that would ordinarily be out of the reach of an entrepreneur if he or she had to buy such market awareness through traditional media.

The Reality Check for your go-to-market strategy includes getting customer feedback on four key elements guiding such a strategy:

- Frequency of purchase

- Amount typically "spent" for each purchase

- Preferred place of purchase

- Preferred information channel for product or service information

Perhaps the most important aspect of this part of the Reality Check is to determine if target customers agree with your channel strategy. For example, do customers want to buy directly from you? Or would they prefer to purchase from an already established channel member, such as a retailer for B2C ventures or an original equipment manufacturer (OEM; a larger firm) or systems integrator for B2B ventures? Remember, a successful channel strategy will accelerate your time to achieve scale. However, the channel strategy must also balance what is best for customers with the cost of implementing that channel at startup. For example, many successful entrepreneurs started first with a regional or "top ten accounts" penetration strategy before expanding to national and then global reach.

We want to emphasize that it is important to get feedback on all of these issues early and make any necessary adjustments now before going to market, since making after-launch changes can be very expensive. The way we do so is by asking customers four simple questions in the Field Research Discussion Guide:

Figure 8.4
HealthyWags
Consolidated Field
Research Data: Go-
to-Market Questions

Question 4: How often do you buy similar products or services? (Open-ended.)

Mother Goose:	Once a month
Dog Mommy:	Once a month
Pet Buddy:	Once every 2 months

Question 5: How much do you spend each time you make a purchase? (Open-ended, but looking for a dollar amount.) Do you prefer to buy, rent, subscribe, etc? (Determine method of payment.)

Mother Goose:	$10
Dog Mommy:	$13
Pet Buddy:	$6

Question 6: Where is the best place to buy products/services such as this? (Open-ended, but look for a specific preferred channel and ways in which they test or try products/services.)

Mother Goose:	Supermarket, Pet Specialty Store
Dog Mommy:	Pet Specialty Store
Pet Buddy:	Supermarket

Question 7: Where do you get your information about products/services such as this? (Open-ended. Look for preferred information sources.)

Mother Goose:	Print, television, friends
Dog Mommy:	Internet, friends
Pet Buddy:	In-store

Question 4: How often do you buy similar products or services?

Mother Goose	Once a month
Dog Mommy	Once a month
Pet Buddy	Once every two months

These data support the team's focus on the female buyers as a startup strategy because they are more diligent, frequent shoppers.

Question 5: How much do you spend each time you make a purchase? [Open ended but look for a dollar amount]

Mother Goose	$10
Dog Mommy	$13
Pet Buddy	$6

These data show that the younger female shoppers—those who view their pets as surrogate children are less price sensitive than the older, primary grocery shopping moms trying to manage a family budget. And for the Boomer males, the Reality Check reveals that they tend to be "cheap" when it comes to buying pet snacks.

Question 6: Where is the best place to buy products/services such as this? [Open ended, but look for a specific preferred channel and ways in which they test or try products/services]

Mother Goose	Supermarket (70%), pet specialty store (10%), Walmart or Target (20%)
Dog Mommy	Supermarket (20%), pet specialty store (50%) including independents, mass merchant (10%), Club store (20%)
Pet Buddy	Supermarket (60%), pet specialty store (10%), Walmart (30%)

Let's say that one of the HealthyWags team members is skeptical of the strength of the specialty channel for younger women – the Dog Mommies. The answer is simply go to several such stores over the weekend and observe who is buying what main meals and snacks. He would find that young women were doing the vast amount of the purchasing, more younger than older, and perhaps a number of young men. We suspect that very few Boomer males would be found shopping the aisles.

The actual HealthyWags team not only did its Reality Check and its in-store ethnography, but also learned the math of channel selection. Grocery chains charge upwards of $2M per set of SKU's, whereas Wholefoods and pet specialty chains do not have such stocking fees. This is another reason why premium products for the premium, specialty channels frequented by young professional women made a lot of sense. Later on, the team could expand to higher end national grocers,

Question 8: Where do you get your information about products/services such as this? [Open ended, but look for preferred information sources]

Mother Goose	Print, television, friends
Dog Mommy	Internet, friends
Pet Buddy	In-store

These data show that Dog Mommy—as a younger consumer—prefers social networking channels of information for new products (as well as services, we find). The traditional Madison Avenue advertising approach (expensive print and broadcast/cable advertisements) for marketing to an older consumer is distrusted by this young consumer. The grocery shopping mom, on the other hand, prefers these traditional information sources—costly for a fledgling company. And Pet Buddy—well, it seems that male pet owners in this Reality Check prefer to be sold to by a knowledgeable sales person because this shopper is simply too lazy to read ingredient panels or grocery advertising.

Testing Your Brand Name

An innovation needs to have a *name*. We recommend that you do this after you ask all the questions to respondents in the Reality Check. If they seem willing, tell them you would like to run a few product or service brand names by them to get their opinions. It is also a fun way to end the interview process! We usually do not do company names in these types of tests—just product and service branding as opposed to the name of the innovation itself. To do a brand name and messaging test:

- Come up with two or three possible brand names for your products or services, and the simple, short, powerful messaging behind these brand names.

- Go onto the Web and find brand names for leading, competing products or services. You might also want to browse the startups in your industry niche and see what they are calling their new products and services. Often, you will find creative new naming. Also look for messaging.

- Have the interviewees first look at what you think are the best competitor brand names. Then have them look at yours. Setting this up as a simple table might be the best approach, with the various competitors' names and messaging in the first column, your possible brand names and messaging in the second column, and the third column open for notes.

The type of responses you are looking for are:

1. Of all the names and messages in the table, which are the clearest and most powerful?

2. If your own brand names and messages "pop," what are the reasons for this? What do they like about your branding?

3. If your brand names and messages seem a little off, what don't they like, and what might they recommend?

4. Please continue to note the type of customer the respondent represents. Different types of customers often react to the same branding in very different ways. Your goal is to develop and validate a brand name and messaging that truly resonate with your target customer.

The Customer Insight
- Seeking ways to show care/love for pet
- Health through nutrition; taste, too
- Snacks should be healthy as main meal
- Local sourcing of food is important, distrusts mass manufacturers

Industry / Segment
- North America: $4B plus
- Big three mass manufacturers: Nestle Purina, Mars, Smuckers
- Lots of snack innovation
- Low volume, very high margin with premium products up to $15/lb

Business Model
- Premium priced
- Specialty stores
- Local manufacturing

Target Customers and Uses
- Primarily young professionals, mostly female but also male
- Shopping for snacks once a month at PetSmart, Petco, or independent. Also some Wholefoods
- Snacks to show care, for rewards, and for training

Positioning
- Functional: best quality, high price
- Emotional: expression of love
- Social: local ,sustainable

Solutions
- All natural, minimally processed
- No byproducts, no leathers
- Artisanal packaging
- Vegetable as well as meat SKUs
- Smaller training bites also
- Engaging Website – story behind products

Summarizing Everything into a Single Template

Figure 8.5 the Innovation Dashboard. This template summarizes all your learning from the Reality Check and the chapters of this book: industry segment and addressable market size, customer group and use, the fundamental customer purchase motivation, the customer benefits and needs (the voice of the customer), the product or service design, and the business model. Combine this with some type of prototype and you have the foundation for a subsequent business plan and pitch for investors or business executives.

Figure 8.5 shows the dashboard applied to the pet snack innovation. The industry segment, its size and growth rate, the target customers and use occasions. In the middle are the customer insight, a persona, and the product/service portfolio. And on the right is the business model, followed by the positioning and branding for the innovation.

All of this, with a few short bullet points, fits on a single page. All the elements should fit together nicely into a coherent, cohesive whole. A simple, clear logic should flow from beginning to end.

The power of summarizing your insights and information on a single page cannot be underestimated. You can quickly show a friend, mentor, or colleague your innovation idea – tested against the market and customers -- and talk about how the different pieces connect and support one another. Some of our students take the poster board approach. Go to Staples. Buy a large, fold-down poster board, and assemble the different pieces of the dashboard on it. And do not forget the pictures of the customers! This brings your audience into the world of your customers. It will make your conversations and presentations all the more real and poignant by addressing the needs and concerns of actual consumers or buying organizations.

READER EXERCISES

As in all our other chapters, we have exercises for you to perform. This set is perhaps the most important because it is a field-based validation of everything you have done so far: target customers and uses, product and service innovations, the revenue side of the business model, and the positioning and branding of your products and services.

Step 1: Edit the Customer Value Proposition for the Reality Check

Finalize your Customer Value Proposition. It should be three or four sentences. Use the examples in the chapter as a guide. You should be able to communicate the essence of your venture to potential customers in about 30 seconds. If you have a drawing or prototype of your product or service idea, include that as an attachment or "show and tell" with the survey. It will make your survey all the more meaningful for respondents. Practice on yourselves first and then on friends outside of your team. Did those friends understand the concept in 30 seconds? If not, keep reworking the text statement until outsiders can clearly understand it.

Also, gather your concept sketches and prototypes. These need to be part of the opening conversation in the Reality Check.

Step 2: Create the Discussion Guide/Survey

Using Figure 8.1 as a reference, prepare your own survey instrument. You should cover all the various bases that are shown in that figure. Once again, practice with teammates and friends outside your team.

Above all, try to keep your survey short and focused. Most customers won't give you much more than 10 minutes for the entire survey itself! But of course, if a consumer or manager in a company wants to talk your ear off about their issues and problems, set the survey aside for a while, listen hard, take notes, and then come back to the survey and wrap things up with a big thank you. Always say thank you to everyone. Let them know that their knowledge and insights are very important for your venture. If they want to stay involved with your project, take their contact information and be sure to follow up. These individuals will help you test your new products or services.

Step 3: Conduct the Field Research

Talk with at least 30 potential customers for each customer group. Why that number? For the ethnography, we suggested between 6 to 12 for observation and in-depth interviewing. This survey has a different purpose. We are trying to validate hypotheses for all your prior customer research. It should be done faster with each customer; and you need more data to have confidence in the results. If you have distinctive customer groups, try to talk to people in each group (e.g., 3 customer groups, 30 each = 90). If you feel that you still have unanswered questions or a lack of clear insight on product/service requirements, positioning, channel, and price, find more prospective customers. Here, the more, the better. We have had student teams talk to a hundred or more prospective customers, and these usually produce the most solid, insightful Reality Checks.

If you are working a B2B market space, you must still try to talk to a sufficient number of managers and users in target corporate customers, perhaps six to eight companies and

Intro: Describe yourself or your company. Do you view yourself as a potential user of this product?	Validate primary and secondary customer groups.
How satisfied are you with the current products/services you use now? *Very dissatisfied Dissatisfied Neither Dis/Sat Satisfied Very Satisfied*	Report percentages. Look for top two box scores: Very Dissatisfied, Dissatisfied.
Do you see the proposed offering as distinctive from the competitors? Not different Somewhat different Highly distinctive	Report percentages. Look for top box scores: Highly Distinctive.
How much would you be willing to pay for this offering compared to current products/services you use now? *A lot less Less Same More A lot more*	Report percentages. Look for top two box scores: More, A lot more.
How often do you buy similar products or services? (Open-ended.)	Report time frequency of purchase.
How much do you spend each time you make a purchase? (Open-ended, but looking for a dollar amount. Try to validate the structure of revenue – e.g. does the customer want to purchase, license, subscribe, try before buy, etc.)	Report money spent range, with average. Report preferred revenue type.
Where is the best place to buy products/services such as this? (Open-ended, but look for a specific preferred channel and ways in which they test or try products/services).	List channels with percentages. Validates go-to-market model.
Where do you get your information about products/services such as this? (Open-ended. Look for preferred information sources.)	List sources with percentages. Validates build awareness model.
How likely is it that you would be willing to buy this offering? Very unlikely Unlikely Neither Likely Very Likely	Report purchase intent. Look for top two box scores: Likely and Very Likely.
What additional features do you think are important in a (product or service) such as this? (Open-ended.)	List the desired features, with most popular & percentages first.
Add your estimation of revenues for a scaled up business (after 5-7 years, or the time cycle appropriate for your industry -- biotech ventures will be much longer.)	This should show your assumptions
Final checklist on key aspects of your venture strategy and business model.	Check them off! Final slide.

Figure 8.6
Reporting the Results of the Reality Check

a couple dozen individuals across those companies. There is no substitute for customer feedback on a structured, systematic Reality Check at this point in time for developing your venture.

Step 4: Analyze and Report the Data

Now begin to analyze what you have discovered. Use Figures 8.6 as a reference for organizing the data and interpreting the results. What do the data tell you? For example, are customers interested in the concept? Are they likely to buy? How much are they likely to spend on each purchase? Through which channel do they prefer to buy your product or service? If you gather a sufficient number of respondents, the data should really tell the strength of customers' preferences for these and other important areas.

First, group the questions into their logical buckets and report percentages for the Likert-type scale questions, e.g., the percentages in each of the 5-point or 3-point scales depending on the question in the Field Discussion Research Guide. Then use major bullet points for the open-ended questions.

Step 5: Create Your Innovation Dashboard

Prepare your dashboard, integrating your strategies and decisions from the successive chapters so far in this book. Use Figure 8.7 as a template. Keep it simple. Use bullet points and short statements. And include a picture or video to bring the target customer and the use case in the dashboard to life. If you have a sketch or a prototype of your new product or service, include that as well as a separate exhibit.

We encourage you to show your results to your trusted advisers, your professors, and your classmates. Have some fun with it! Nobody comes back from the field without a few surprises.

Figure 8.7
The Innovation
Dashboard Template

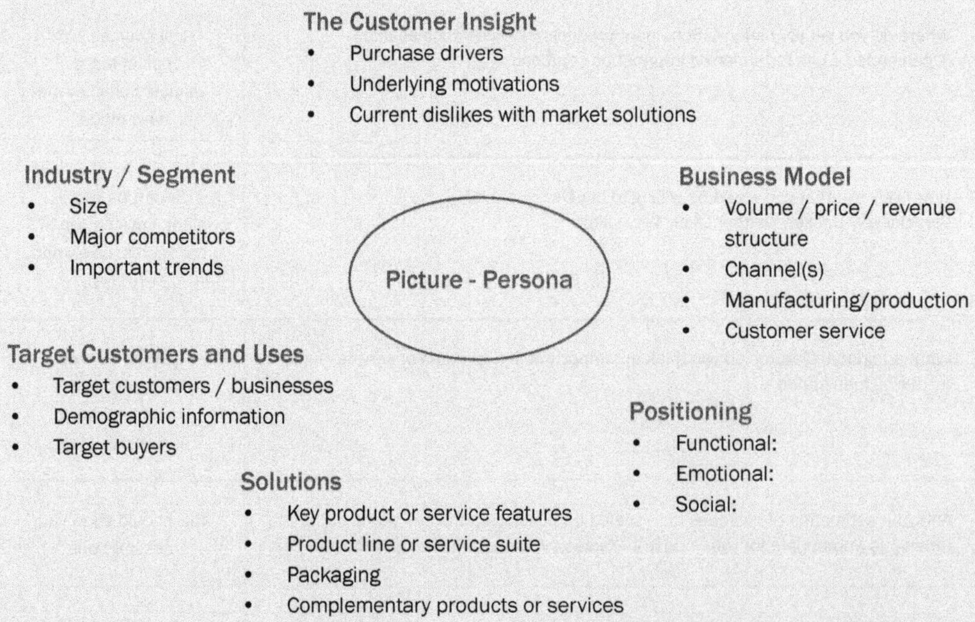

The Customer Insight
- Purchase drivers
- Underlying motivations
- Current dislikes with market solutions

Industry / Segment
- Size
- Major competitors
- Important trends

Picture - Persona

Business Model
- Volume / price / revenue structure
- Channel(s)
- Manufacturing/production
- Customer service

Target Customers and Uses
- Target customers / businesses
- Demographic information
- Target buyers

Positioning
- Functional:
- Emotional:
- Social:

Solutions
- Key product or service features
- Product line or service suite
- Packaging
- Complementary products or services

If you are not satisfied with your findings, do what many other innovators have done before you: pivot! Do a quick revision of your target customer and use, the product or services strategy, the business model, and the positioning—create a new Customer Value Proposition, a modified product or service design, a business model, and then do the survey again. We have seen teams turn tough situations completely around in a matter of weeks and go on to launch successful innovations. You can do it, too.

Final Thoughts

A market and customer tested innovation is a lot more than most first-time innovators have in their arsenal before thinking about how to commercialize the innovation in the form of a new company or a new part of an existing business. We hope you now realize the power of your industry and customer insights and how they set you apart from those many other would-be innovators who just "wing it".

There are many other books you can read for business planning needed to commercialize an innovation, including ours. However, the foundation of any startup or corporate venture is itself a well considered and customer vetted innovation – and that is precisely what you have learned how to accomplish with the methods of this book. We hope you have not only learned, but also had some fun applying the methods, and worked your way towards a great result! And if you want to learn more, go to our Website, www.instituteforenterprisegrowth.com, for additional books, templates, cases, videos, and more – all centered on the themes of product, service, and business model innovation.

Thank you for participating in our journey to innovate. It is our deepest and most sincere hope the lessons learned here will serve you, your customers, and society well beyond this course and throughout the years ahead.

AUTHORS'
BIOGRAPHY

Marc H. Meyer is the Robert J. Shillman Professor of Entrepreneurship and the Matthews Distinguished Professor of Business at Northeastern University where he started the Entrepreneurship and Innovation Group within the D'Amore McKim School of Business. Northeastern is now ranked as one of the leading undergraduate entrepreneurship programs in the United States, with an emphasis on experiential entrepreneurial learning with its Co-op and on-campus venture acceleration programs.

Dr. Meyer is a widely published author in the field of innovation and technology management. In this book, *Venturing: Innovation and Business Planning for Entrepreneurs*, Dr. Meyer speaks from experience. He has been part of the start-up teams of three software companies (two of which were acquired) and is actively involved with early stage firms as an investor and board member. Moreover, the methods used in this book have helped numerous students and young alumni launch new companies at Northeastern and other universities.

Dr. Meyer is a graduate of Harvard and holds a Master's and Ph.D. from M.I.T. While a graduate student in his mid-20s, he worked with MIT friends to build his first software company (VenturCom, later Ardence, then acquired by acquired by Citrix). Since that time he has ventured and consulted across many industries, including medical devices and software, consumer products, industrial equipment, and computing in many different forms. He has been a Visiting Professor and Scientist at M.I.T. and a Visiting Professor at Delft Technical University. In addition to his work in industry, Dr. Meyer serves on the Board of the National Wildlife Refuge Association.

Frederick G. Crane is an Executive Professor of Entrepreneurship & Innovation at the College of Business at Northeastern University; Editor of the *Journal of the Academy of Business Education*. He was formerly a professor of marketing and entrepreneurship at the University of New Hampshire and a Chair and Full Professor at Dalhousie University. In addition to his academic publications, Dr. Crane is the author of widely used marketing textbooks in both corporate and entrepreneurial contexts. Dr. Crane is also an award-winning educator who has received numerous honors for teaching excellence over the past 20 years.

Dr. Crane grew up in a family business and also started and operated several of his own businesses, including successful management consulting and research firms. Dr. Crane is a co-founder of Ceilidh Insights, a consumer insight research company serving numerous corporate clients. He has also been an angel investor and has worked as a consultant for angel investors, venture capitalists, and government agencies on venture funding projects.

Dr. Crane lives on a farm with his beloved horses and dogs. One of his major passions is equine rescue especially the welfare of wild mustangs.

Lightning Source UK Ltd.
Milton Keynes UK
UKOW07f1142091116

287217UK00002B/26/P